For the Record

Recording Skills Training Manual

Liz O'Rourke

Consultant editor Neil Thompson

Russell House Publishing

First published in 2002 by:
Russell House Publishing Ltd.
4 St George's House
Uplyme Road
Lyme Regis
Dorset DT7 3LS

Tel: 01297-443948
Fax: 01297-442722
e-mail: help@russellhouse.co.uk

British Library Cataloguing-in-publication Data:
A catalogue record for this book is available from the British Library.

ISBN: 1-903855-01-2

Typeset by TW Typesetting, Plymouth, Devon

Printed by Bath Press, Bath

Russell House Publishing

Is a group of social work, probation, education and youth and community work practitioners and academics working in collaboration with a professional publishing team.
Our aim is to work closely with the field to produce innovative and valuable materials to help managers, trainers, practitioners and students.
We are keen to receive feedback on publications and new ideas for future projects.

Acknowledgements

I am grateful to many people for their support and suggestions in the writing of this manual. When I first embarked on this area of training some years ago, I was filled with a degree of apprehension. I did not feel I was very much of an expert and I severely doubted my ability to make such a subject engaging and enjoyable. However, through working with learners and discussing their concerns and experiences, I have developed a confidence and enthusiasm which I hope I can share, through this manual, with others taking on a training remit for recording skills. I owe a great debt to all the many learners who have helped widen my knowledge and deepen my understanding.

I should also like to acknowledge Norman Mark, a specialist in social care staff training, who kindly shared with me The Four Columns Evaluation which appears in Section 4, and the work of Graham Hopkins, whose book, *Plain English for Social Services* is referred to in Section 5.

Various people have been involved in looking at different draft sections of the manual and I have been very grateful for their comments and suggestions. They include:

- Shirley Barefield: Inspector with the Inspection and Regulation Unit, Residential Care, Berkshire.
- Brian Barefield: Senior lecturer and course leader, Access to Social Work, West Thames College, NVQ lecturer and assessor for foster care, Hounslow, Ealing, Hammersmith and Fulham Social Services.
- Margaret Mitchell: CCETSW Assessor and External Examiner, NVQ External Verifier.
- Charlotte Salveson: Trainer in social work and social care.
- Janet Wignall: Senior social worker, Wokingham Social Services.

A special thanks must go to Professor Neil Thompson who has worked closely with me in an advisory role. He has been constructive and positive throughout and I am very grateful for all his encouragement.

I would finally like to thank Betty Wackerbarth, Director of BASE Cymru, to whom this manual is dedicated. Long after her official retirement, she continues to work with tireless energy and enthusiasm in the cause of improving standards of care through staff development and training. It was she, who first persuaded me to develop recording skills as a specialist area of training. Betty continues to be a source of inspiration to all who work with her.

For Betty — a very remarkable lady

Contents

Section 1: Introduction

This Pack is designed to be used with social care workers, employed in a range of settings with different client groups.

The Pack can be used by experienced trainers and also those with less formal training experience. It is sufficiently flexible to be used within the context of supervision and team meetings as well as organised training programmes.

The intention of the pack is to provide material which will stimulate an awareness of the importance of recording in the delivery of quality care, as well as identifying the principles of effective recording practice.

The case material includes scenarios relevant to those working with older people, adults with learning and physical disabilities and mental health problems, as well as those working with children. Although the main focus is on those providing direct care, there are exercises which would be useful to both student and qualified social workers. The suggested training programmes are specifically aimed at providing social workers with an opportunity to review their practice in the light of current guidelines on effective recording.

Why recording skills are important

The pack has developed from my experience of delivering training on recording skills to many different groups of workers. When I was originally approached about tutoring such programmes, I have to admit to having not been overly enthusiastic. Recording skills did not seem the most lively or interesting area of training to be involved with. But the more I explored the potential of the subject through a succession of courses, with a range of learners, the more I became aware of the powerful influence such training might have.

Recording skills are less about writing ability, and far more about being able to observe and listen, to take in information, process it and interpret it, while still being clear about how much your own subjective perception and understanding may be influencing the way in which you then describe to others what you believe you have seen and heard. As a sociologist, I am all too aware of how each individual can assume that the sense they make of the world, the meaning they give to their experiences, is somehow an objective fact, and that people do not always sufficiently realise how that same world can be looked at in very different ways.

Workers are in a powerful position to define the reality of the caring situation in their terms, to describe it from their perspective and to believe that their professional expertise ensures their objectivity. Service users, by virtue of their very disadvantage in requiring help and support, may find it extremely difficult to put forward any alternative to the way in which their situation has been described and defined by professionals.

Social care work has become more focused on the service user in recent years. The emphasis is on designing services around the needs of service users. The basic principles and values of social care work are concerned with respecting the individual and involving them in the process of devising the care package. Open access has encouraged workers to be more aware of how they record. It can still be hard, however, to hear the voices of service users, to feel that **their** perspective is actually reflected in the written record.

This pack is very much about encouraging workers to reflect on how problematic it can be in writing a record which is both objective and reliable, where the service user's perspective is included in the account and where the worker's judgement is clearly identified as such. I wanted to design a series of exercises and activities which would both enable workers to understand the problematic nature of recording, and provide them with an opportunity to look at how they might improve their own recording skills and write more effective records.

Recording skills training has become a greater priority because of increasing concern over both the legal implications of recording, and the impact of recording on the quality of care delivered. More and more staff, who have never previously been involved in recording are having to contribute to the writing of careplans and to case recording. It is therefore vital that learning opportunities be made available to encourage workers to develop their skills and their confidence.

My approach to training is highly participative. I want learners to feel actively involved in the process of learning, to engage with me in looking at why and how they might think and do things differently. I have tried to incorporate that approach into this training pack. I want to encourage learners to reflect on the ideas presented, join in with discussion and explore the implications for their own practice.

What the pack covers

The general learning aim is to help learners improve their recording skills and write more accurately, clearly, concisely and appropriately.

The overall objectives are to:

- Understand the importance of recording in providing quality care.
- Appreciate the need for confidentiality and understand the implications of recording.
- Know and apply the principles of good recording practice.
- To identify the problems in recordings, i.e. selective perception, failing to distinguish fact from opinion and the use of value laden language.
- Understand the purpose of different systems of recording.

Each section of the pack has its own specific learning objectives.

Recording skills and legislation

The pack has been written within the legal framework of the Data Protection Act 1998. The pack is concerned with recording practice and does not attempt to look at the specific legal framework of childcare or mental health, although there is a specific reference to the particular information which should be held in respect of children and young people in residential care.

It is further acknowledged that there will be variations in the legal context between England and Wales and Scotland, which again the pack does not specifically address.

Recording skills and care planning

Recording skills inevitably impinge on care planning, and the need for further training in recording skills often arises because staff are now more actively involved in care planning. Reference is made to the care planning process within the pack, although the emphasis is, for the most part, on recording.

What the pack does not cover

Literacy issues

Over the years I have encountered various learners sent on recording skills training because they had very basic problems with reading and writing. This arises from a fundamental misunderstanding over what recording skills training is actually concerned with. Yes, there is some attention given to how one actually writes, particularly in relation to the value of using plain language, but if someone has real difficulties with basic literacy, then a one-day programme is not going to address needs that twelve years of compulsory schooling have failed to meet. Such problems need to be handled sensitively. People need to be reassured that such difficulties can be experienced by many people, including successful people, running their own businesses, and that there are sources of help available.

The telephone number of the National Helpline of the Basic Skills Agency is 0800 700 987, who can provide information on the adult literacy provision in any given local area, which may include colleges and a range of private and voluntary agencies. Tuition and support can be provided in small groups, where programmes can be tailored to meet individual needs.

Specific agency forms and systems

This pack is designed to look at recording issues in general. Every agency has its own particular system of paperwork, with specific forms and documentation for different purposes. Guidelines on the use of particular forms have inevitably to be agency-based. It is important to emphasise that whatever the precise form being used, the general principles of effective recording practice apply.

Guidance in using the pack

The Pack is divided into Sections. Section Two suggests ways of devising and structuring training programmes, and Sections Three to Eight contain the basic component parts, covering a range of topics, from which the reader, be they manager or trainer, can build the training programme which they need.

Each Section of the Pack is divided into manageable chunks, called Training Modules. The training modules cover a wide range of topics, and come in several varieties: some are merely informative, whilst others require active involvement of the learners by way of practical exercises. Most modules therefore have accompanying exercise sheets, handouts, overhead transparencies, or case sheets.

To help you navigate around the manual the various activities or materials have been assigned their own particular icon. At the start of each training module you will find:

 The objective of the module.

 The time required for the module.

 The materials needed to run the module.

 Trainer's guidelines on running the module.

At the end of the modules are the special materials that you will need to run that particular module:

| OHT | Overhead transparencies (OHTs)

| Handouts (HOs)

✓ Exercises

Some of the modules also contain case sheets and role-play scenarios to help understanding and give a degree of realism.

Sections Three, Four and Five contain training modules which cover the basic principles of observation, learning and recording, and which are consequently intended as the foundations of one or two-day training programmes.

Section Six contains a number of case studies which can be used to practice various ways of recording information.

Section Seven contains advanced training modules, with exercises more demanding and complex in the issues they present, for use with those who have already worked through the earlier material, or for higher level courses.

Section Eight has modules particularly for management and supervisory staff.

In modules which have accompanying case sheets, there are different versions for use by different learner groups; for example, for those working with older people, the storyline on the case sheet will concern those working with older people, and so on. (It should be noted that, although the case material may contain names, dates and locations, this detail is fictional, and is included only because it is necessary for such detail to be put into records.)

Thus it should be possible, by mixing and matching training modules, and choosing the appropriate version of the accompanying case or exercise sheet, to construct short or long training programmes with material which is relevant to learners' needs and working environments.

While the modules do contain Trainer's Guidelines in respect of timing, these are approximate and can vary depending on the size of the group and the degree to which they engage in discussion. I have tried to produce material which can be used by experienced trainers and by those, including many managers, who are not so experienced in the training role. The guidelines are there to provide a basis for planning and organising a programme, but the pack can be used in as flexible a way as needed. Some modules could be used in a one-to-one supervision session and some can be used within the context of a team meeting. Effective learning can occur in many different situations.

I have also taken the decision to include fairly detailed notes of the points I believe should be included in feedback and discussion. Furthermore I have provided 'model' or 'suggested' records for certain exercises. These are not necessarily meant to be definitive, but I feel it is my responsibility to at least offer anyone using the pack some indication of what the record should look like. Such 'suggested' recordings should be regarded as a guide and not necessarily the 'correct' or 'prescribed' answer.

Section 2: Organising and Structuring Training Programmes

Introduction

This section sets out some outline training programmes of varying duration, incorporating the different exercises in the manual with advice on group size and time allowance.

The suggested programmes assume four sessions of approximately the same length through the day, starting at 9.30 a.m. and finishing at 4.30 p.m., with normal refreshment and lunch breaks:

9.30	Introductions
10.00	Session 1
11.00	Coffee
11.15	Session 2
12.30	Lunch
1.30	Session 3
3.00	Tea
3.15	Session 4
4.30	Close

Each session will comprise one or more training modules, which are included in this pack. A training module will normally deal with one or more topics of interactive learning promoted by the trainer using handouts, visual aids, or exercises.

Basic one-day course for care providers or day one of a two-day course

This may comprise:

Session 1

Welcome and Introductory module (p9) from Section 2: How to start the programme
The first three modules from Section 3: Selective perception

Session 2

Module from Section 5: Why, what, and how do we record?
Module from Section 5: A day in the life of . . .
Module from Section 4: Where does the information go?

Session 3

Module from Section 3: Being positively objective
Module from Section 5: Recording guidelines, confidentiality and right to access

Session 4

Module from Section 5: The daily log
Module from Section 6: Your witness . . . making a record from role-play

I have also run the basic one-day course where Session 3 is more concentrated, leaving time to include The daily log. Session 4 can then cover Your witness . . . and For the purpose of . . . Timings are necessarily quite difficult to predict and will depend very much on the amount of discussion generated.

Follow-up course for care providers or day two of a two-day course

This may comprise:

Session 1

Welcome back, or welcome, and Introductory module (p9) from Section 2: How to start the programme
The recording skills questionnaire (p10) should either be completed on the second morning of the two-day course, or distributed and completed before the follow-up course, and discussed as part of a review of practice since the first course.
Module from Section 6: Making a record from transcripts

Session 2

Module from Section 4: The four columns evaluation
Module from Section 4: Principles of effective recording systems

Session 3

Module from Section 5: 'Plain English'
Module from Section 6: For the purpose of . . .

Session 4

Module from Section 7: The record as evidence
Review and action plans

One-day course for social workers or care managers

This may comprise:

Session 1

Welcome and Introductory module (p9) from Section 2: How to start the programme.
The first three modules from Section 3: Selective perception

Session 2

Module from Section 5: Why, what, and how do we record?
Module from Section 5: Recording guidelines, confidentiality and the right to access
Transcripts

It is anticipated that the informative sessions will take less time with this group.

Session 3

Module from Section 3: Being positively objective
Module from Section 5: Plain English
Module from Section 5: Principles of effective recording systems
Module from Section 4: The four columns evaluation

There will be insufficient time to actually complete this last exercise, but the idea is to explain it so that the participants are able to take it back to their own teams and use it to review their systems.

Session 4

Module from Section 7: Assessing needs
Review and action plans

These are suggested outlines only. The material and exercises set out in the training modules in this pack are sufficiently flexible as to be organised in various combinations. The important point is to identify what are the particular needs of your learners and arrange the material accordingly.

Introductory module: How to start the programme

I am assuming at least half an hour at the beginning of each programme for introductions and identification of learning expectations and objectives. This helps participants to feel more comfortable with one another and with you, as well as helping them better understand what the programme will involve.

The suggested format is to:

- Introduce yourself and say a little about the background of the course.
- Pair each participant with someone they do not know, or know less well in the group, and ask them to briefly interview their partner in order to introduce them to the rest of the group. Everyone is asked to think about their expectations of the day as part of this introductory exercise.
- Each participant is introduced by their partner and learning expectations are noted by the trainer.
- The expectations are then reviewed in terms of the actual course programme and learning objectives. If there is any mismatch, it is useful to take the opportunity to clarify any misunderstanding or confusion and suggest or discuss with individuals later how specific individual learning expectations might be met, e.g. adult literacy.
- Ground rules can be drawn up at this stage, although I think there is always a danger of this becoming something of a ritual on many courses. I prefer to simply draw people's attention to the importance of punctuality and respect for one another, as well as stating that my own style as a trainer is informal, welcoming and encouraging of participants' contributions and participation.

Recording skills questionnaire

This questionnaire has been designed to help evaluate your previous learning in respect of Recording Skills and to assess your further learning needs.

1. Why is recording important?

2. How do you judge the amount of detail you need to include in a recording in order to be both accurate and relevant, as well as being concise and complete?

3. What has been the main change in respect of third party information with the recent Data Protection Act 1998?

4. What criticisms would you make of the following recordings?
a. Daniel appeared worried

b. Sheila has been acting up all night. She's really done my head in.

c. Mrs Shaw has been very unco-operative and appears determined to obstruct all efforts to help her.

Section 3: Selective Perception

Introduction

This section is concerned with introducing some of the main problems in making sense of what we hear and observe, and includes information on the subjective factors influencing perception. The modules in this section are basic to most courses or training programmes, where they form the first session of the day, and should introduce learners to the problematic nature of information and how we understand it.

Even before we attempt to record our observations, we need to be aware of just how difficult it is to be clear about what we are looking at or hearing, before going on to process and interpret that information, so that we have made sense of it.

The first three modules are all exercises, can follow one another, and will usually take just over an hour. They could be used separately but they will have much greater impact if run together.

The later module involves case material.

Training module: What is information?

↗ Objective

The aim of this module is to encourage participants to think about how much and how many different kinds of information they process every day.

🕐 Timing

Allow 20 minutes for this exercise.

✎ Materials

You will need:

- flipchart paper
- marker pens for each group member
- bluetack or masking tape
- Trainer's prompt list: *Visual, aural and written information* (p14)

ⓘ Trainer's guidelines

Step 1: allow 5 minutes

Introduce the exercise. Split the group into three smaller groups. Give them each a piece of flipchart paper and a marker pen. Explain that each group will have a different type of information to concentrate on:

1. Group A: visual information, i.e. information which relies solely on a visual image and not on any written words or numbers.
2. Group B: aural information, i.e. information that relies solely on sounds.
3. Group C: written information, i.e. information concerned with written words or numbers.

The participants are asked to write down on the flipchart paper as many different examples, from both outside and inside work, as they can identify of their group's particular type of information.

Step 2: allow 10 minutes

The three groups record their examples on flipchart paper. Some groups may need a little encouragement in terms of what they are required to do, and it may be helpful to suggest a few ideas as prompts to get them started. The Trainer's Prompt List below may help here. You should acknowledge that some examples could fall into more than one group. For example, maps often rely on a combination of written and visual information, though it is possible to have a map without any written words. Similarly clocks or watches could fall into all three groups, as we usually rely on reading the clock face according to the position of the hands in relation to the numbers. We can also tell the time by the chimes of a clock, and because the clock face is such a familiar image, we can even tell the time by a watch without any numbers.

It is not expected that all items in the Trainer's Prompt List should be included, but the general idea of the exercise is to stimulate participants to think as widely and imaginatively as possible.

Step 3: allow 5 minutes

Look at each piece of flipchart paper in turn and run through the different examples, either reading them yourself or asking a group representative to do so.

Put all three sheets on the wall where participants can view them together. make the point that we rarely think about how much information we are constantly taking in, and the effort that goes into processing it and making sense of it. perhaps we become a little more aware of ourselves in a less familiar environment, e.g. a foreign country, where we can no longer take things so much for granted, but for the most part we remain unaware of the complex business of information processing.

Trainer's prompt list: Visual, aural and written information

Visual information	Aural information	Written information
clothing	alarm clock	newspapers
uniforms	kitchen appliances:	e-mails
body language	• kettle ⎫ clicks	books
facial expression	• toaster ⎬ whistles	timetables
gestures	• microwave ⎭ pings	magazines
physical appearance:	shower	road signs
• pallor	toilet flushing	lists
• sweating	letterbox	circulars
• racial origin	doorbell	bills
signs:	knocker	directories
• road	keys	receipts
• directional	door lock	labels
• warning	traffic noises:	calendars
• toilet	• trains	brochures
colours:	• aeroplanes	leaflets
• traffic lights	birdsong	diaries
• yellow and black hazard	telephone ring	posters
• red and blue taps for	voices:	memos
water	• accent	instructions
• funeral black	• tone	pay slips
• zebra crossing	snoring	bank statements
• wiring in a plug	coughing	pension books
• emergency vehicle lights	wheezing	passports
disability indicators:	groaning	tickets
• white stick	breathing	menus
icons:	crying	letters
• computer	laughing	forms
• maps	shouting	wills
• diagrams	stamping	certificates
religious and cultural logos:	footsteps	CVs
• cross	clapping	clocks
• crescent	crashes	stamps
• national symbols	bangs	teletext
• flags	slamming doors	car number plates
sign language	crossing bleeper	charts
adverts	sirens	greeting cards
pictures	alarms	money
cartoons	weather sounds:	speedometers
photos	• wind	programmes
	• rain	
	animal noises:	
	• growling	
	• barking	
	• whimpering	
	morse code	

Training module: Listening styles

⬈ Objective

The aim of this exercise is to consider how and why people will comprehend the same message differently.

🕐 Timing

Allow 20 minutes for this exercise.

✎ Materials

You will need:

- paper
- pens
- handout: HO1, *The listening styles model*

ⓘ Trainer's guidelines

Step 1: allow 4 minutes

Explain that you are going to look at the problems involved in the type of information exchange which we rely on most: talking with other people. Ask participants why they think a group of people may all hear someone say the same thing but each go away with a slightly different version of what they think they have heard.

Answers may include:

- Different levels of concentration or attention.
- Different feelings or attitudes toward the speaker.
- Different experiences which influence the degree of insight or empathy you have with the speaker.
- Different ideas about relevance and interest.
- Different levels of existing knowledge, experience, understanding, which may make new information more or less difficult to process and understand.
- Concentration on those parts which reinforce or support our own ideas.

Acknowledge that all of these answers are undoubtedly important, but suggest that something else may be going on and that to demonstrate this, you will use some role play.

Explain that you are going to be 'Terry' (or make up a name) and that you work in an office and are responsible for the coffee money. Ask the participants to listen to what you are saying to think about how they feel about you and what they think is going to happen, for instance, will you carry on being responsible for the coffee money?

Step 2: allow 2 minutes

Sit on a chair facing the group and go into your role. Say how you didn't really want the job in the first place but it was typical that no one else could be bothered, so you got lumbered with it. You didn't mind in the beginning because it had all been agreed how much everyone would put in. But since then, people have come back with all sorts of excuses about why they haven't got the right money and you are really fed up with having to put your hand in your own pocket. And it's not as if there is any gratitude, because they are always moaning that it's not the right sort of tea, they want herbal teas and decaffeinated coffee and I don't know how many different kinds of milk! And they want biscuits! Well, you are really fed up with it all.

Step 3: allow 4 minutes

Divide into groups of three or four participants. Ask each group to discuss the questions you posed. Reassure them that there is no right or wrong answer and, where there is disagreement within a group, that they need to feed that back afterwards.

Step 4: allow 5 minutes

Ask groups to feed back. The range of responses will vary but usually there are a number who will feel 'Terry' is a complete pain, a 'professional moaner', and if it wasn't the coffee money, it would be something else. Some may see him as attention seeking, enjoying the status or importance of the responsibility or position, power mad. Some may feel there is a lack of assertiveness skills or organising ability, and that Terry just needs to be given the skills he lacks. Others may feel very sympathetic, feeling that he is being taken advantage of. Someone may feel Terry is just having a bit of an 'off' day, while others may feel the coffee money is simply a symptom of a much deeper, unresolved problem in Terry's life. Even if you do not get this whole range, you can point to the potential variety of responses.

It is important to treat the responses in a fairly light-hearted way, but to still underline that it demonstrates how people react differently, and then suggest that some of those differences can be explained in terms of a simple model.

Step 5: allow 5 minutes

Distribute the handout, HO1, *The listening styles model*, and discuss the different types of listener. In addition, ask participants to think about how difficult it is for each of these to communicate with one another. In response to someone saying, 'I'm alright, really, I am . . .' (sniff):

- The **literal listener** says, 'Well, they said they were alright, didn't they?'
- The **emotional listener** says, 'Can't you see that they were really upset?'
- The **meaning listener** says, 'Can't you see that was all put on for effect, I know what their game is.'

People are capable of moving between styles, but most of us do tend to have a dominant style that we instinctively adopt. Ask the participants if they can recognise people they know, or themselves, in these different styles.

This exercise is meant to be light hearted, but nevertheless demonstrates how difficult it is to be sure that we have always heard people accurately, without our own selective perception obscuring or complicating the message.

▣ HO1: The listening styles model

1. The literal listener

The **literal listener** concentrates on the exact words that people use and will often be able to quote verbatim; they are concerned with detail, are very precise, direct and up front with people, and expect people to be up front with them. The literal listener does not like vagueness, ambiguity or confusion, and, if there is ever any disagreement over what is supposed to have been said, will say, 'But you said . . .'

2. The emotional listener

The **emotional listener** is less interested in the exact words that people use, but is far more concerned with how someone appears to be feeling. The emotional listener will note tone of voice, facial expression, body language and any discontinuity between the verbal, and non-verbal, communication.

3. The meaning listener

The **meaning listener** works from the almost opposite premise of the literal listener, and believes that the most important part of any message is not what is being said, but the hidden message or agenda. Meaning listeners assume that people rarely say what they really mean, and that it is important to look beyond the words, to work out what lies behind the message.

Theses different styles all have their own strengths and weaknesses:

- The **literal listener** is very precise, direct and up front, but may sometimes be rather rigid and lacking in imagination.
- The **emotional listener** can be very empathic, but may also sometimes be overly gullible.
- The **meaning listener** is often alert to subtle messages, but may sometimes read things into messages that are not there, and miss what is actually being said. At its most extreme, this style can border on paranoia!

Training module: Powers of observation

⬈ Objective

The aim of this module is to highlight the different ways in which people may express different physical states and emotions.

🕐 Timing

Allow 20 minutes for this exercise.

✏️ Materials

You will need:

- overhead projector (OHP)
- overhead transparency: OHT1 *Powers of observation*

OR

- put the information on a flipchart

ⓘ Trainer's guidelines

This entire exercise should be approached as a whole-group activity where everyone is invited to contribute and to discuss the ideas presented.

Step 1: allow 10 minutes

Show your prepared OHT1, revealing each item in turn. Select about six of the bulleted points that are most appropriate for the work settings of your participants. Ask the group how they would recognise someone in this state, for example, in pain or discomfort. They should be precise, for instance, if they say 'facial expression', ask exactly what sort of facial expression.

   For each item, there should be a range of, and indeed conflicting and contradictory signs, indicating the same physical state or emotion, e.g. 'pain or discomfort' could be indicated by:

- pale skin colour
- flushed skin colour
- drawing attention to the part of the body that hurts
- facial grimace of pain
- crying
- moaning
- remaining very quiet and withdrawn
- becoming restless
- becoming irritable
- becoming aggressive

Shyness might be indicated by:

- timidity
- avoiding eye contact
- anxiousness

- hesitancy
- reserve
- withdrawal
- offishness
- aloofness
- extroversion, compensating for shyness
- someone being the life and soul of the party
- the fool who performs to avoid their shyness

Aggressiveness might by indicated by:

- a sarcastic or pointed remark
- silence
- staring
- walking out
- pointing a finger
- shaking a fist or object
- a raised voice
- shouting
- swearing
- slamming doors
- banging or kicking objects or furniture
- throwing objects
- breaking objects
- threatening to or using a weapon
- hitting
- biting
- scratching
- punching

Step 2: allow 10 minutes

Always use 'aggressiveness' as the last example so that you can go on to ask about their perception of these different behaviours, all of which are described as aggressive.

You may want to take a small detour and look at 'verbal abuse' or 'swearing' and ask what words or language they would include in these terms. There is often a rather coy response to this question. Ask if they perceive a qualitative difference between:

- 'You're just a bloody fool . . .'
- 'Fuck off, you old slag . . .'

You need to make the point that in relation to abuse, both swearing and other forms of 'aggression', people will have different thresholds of what they take offence at and what upsets them, and which influences the way they then describe the behaviour.

After this, ask the participants whether they consider describing someone as 'aggressive' is a statement of fact or opinion. Explain in relation to all the different examples they have previously given of aggressive behaviour, why the term is unhelpful, indicating more about the response of the observer than the actual behaviour.

Suggest that a more factual description would focus on the actual behaviour and the words used.

How would you recognise someone who was:

- in pain or discomfort
- anxious
- frightened
- sad or depressed
- grieving
- shy
- lonely
- ashamed or guilty
- bored
- tired
- aggressive

Training module: Being positively objective

↗ Objective

The aim of this module is to illustrate the power of language in influencing the way we perceive people and the way in which our accounts can influence colleagues. The module asks learners to compare two accounts of the same service user, written by two different workers, one being more positive than the other. In version A, the account attempts to understand the individual service user's perspective. In version B, the account is more detached and tends to reduce the individual to another *case* or *problem*. Learners are encouraged to go beyond a simple distinction between version A as good, and version B as bad. Instead they are asked to think about how those two versions would affect the way in which the service users would be viewed by other workers, and the way in which future work would be planned.

There are different versions, and different case sheets, for those working with different client groups. The Trainer's guidelines illustrate one version, *Vera Miles*, and for each of the other versions, trainers should follow the same procedure, but incorporate the details set out on the relevant case sheet.

🕐 Timing

Allow 30 minutes for this exercise.

✎ Materials

You will need:

- case sheets, *Being positively objective*:
  - 1A: Older people. Vera Miles
  - 1B: Children and young people. Charlie Harris
  - 1C: Learning disability. Mary Saunders
  - 1D: Physical disability. Trevor Hutton
  - 1E: Mental health problems. Mehmet Erman
- flipchart
- marker pens

ⓘ Trainer's guidelines

Step 1: allow approximately 15 minutes

Divide the participants into small groups of two, three or four individuals. Give them a copy of the relevant case sheet. Ask them to read it through individually and then to discuss collectively, how the two versions compare. What does each version tell them about the service user described and the two workers responsible for the descriptions?

Step 2: allow approximately 15 minutes

Each group is asked to give a summary of their discussions; the main points can be written up on the flipchart. Feedback can be interestingly diverse. Some may feel that version A is too rosy, the sort of description you may get when a social worker is trying to persuade you to take an individual into your establishment. Some may feel that in its very detachment, version B is more factual and objective. It will be important to draw attention to some of the judgemental words in version B, e.g. aggressive, disruptive, moody, argumentative, volatile, dominant, irritable, unco-operative, aimlessly wandering.

Most will feel that the worker in version A has tried to get to know the service user and provides a more positive basis on which to work with the person, while the worker in version B sees the service user more in terms of the problems they present. It is almost possible to hear the service user's voice in Version A, although version B may also contain some valuable information, e.g. Miss Miles not only prefers one-to-one contact, but becomes very upset and agitated when placed in large groups.

The trainer can then ask the group as a whole how would they feel about the individual service user if they had only read version B and what consequences that might have for the way they then approached that person. The significance of self-fulfilling prophecies, (i.e. people often behave the way they feel others expect them to behave) can be introduced into the discussion.

The discussion should conclude with the trainer emphasising the importance of providing an account which is factual and which tries to give the reader the opportunity of understanding the service user in their own terms, while also providing a basis for working positively and constructively with that person.

Being positively objective. Case sheet 1A, Older people: Vera Miles

Version A

Miss Vera Miles, aged 81, is a quiet lady who has recently moved from sheltered accommodation into residential care. Although very reluctant to leave her flat, her increasing confusion was putting her at considerable risk. She was diagnosed with Alzheimer's Disease eight years ago. Miss Miles has no family, although she does frequently ask for her mother, who died when she was twelve. She worked as a librarian for many years and was an active member of the Ramblers' Association. If prompted, she enjoys talking about the past.

Miss Miles has suffered from arthritis for over fifteen years, which has particularly affected her fingers and hands. She is still otherwise very mobile and spends a lot of time walking around the building. Despite her confusion, she seems to be settling in to her new home, smiling at staff and other residents, and relating well to her keyworker, who she now appears to recognise. Miss Miles responds positively to one-to-one social contact, but can become anxious in larger groups or in more noisy environments.

Miss Miles needs help with personal care, but likes to choose her clothes if given the opportunity. She needs some assistance when using the toilet, but occasionally does not always give sufficient warning to get there in time.

Being positively objective. Case sheet 1A, Older people: Vera Miles

Version B

Miss Miles is aged 81, single with no family. She suffers from Alzheimers' Disease, arthritis and a degree of incontinence. She recently moved from sheltered accommodation where she posed too serious a risk to herself and others. She spends long periods aimlessly wandering around the building, frequently calls for her dead mother, has poor short-term memory and lacks orientation to time and place. She requires personal care and toileting. She has been assigned a keyworker. Miss Miles becomes very agitated with large groups of people, sometimes shouting and shrieking during social activities.

Being positively objective. Case sheet 1B, Children and young people: Charlie Harris

Version A

Charlie (as he prefers to be called) Harris is now fifteen and has spent the last seven years in foster or residential care. There have been attempts to reunite him with his mother, but her dependence on drugs has always led to her breaking down and not being able to cope. Charlie has become very upset when these attempted reunions have failed, feeling that he is responsible. He still wants to return to his mother and has not been able to accept foster care as an alternative.

Charlie is a bright and intelligent boy, whose early school reports indicated great potential. He was especially keen on creative writing, but since moving to senior school, he has found the discipline of school life increasingly difficult to cope with. He formed a positive relationship with the English teacher and would regularly attend his lessons, while truanting from most others. However since that teacher moved to another job, Charlie has lost all interest.

Charlie has recently been picked up by the police, once for shoplifting and once for joy-riding. Charlie says he was just having a laugh with his mates, they were daring one another. Charlie is adamant that he wants nothing to do with smoking or drugs after seeing the damage they have done to his mother. He says he likes a drink but he's only got drunk once.

Charlie says he finds it difficult to get on with the other young people in the home. He feels they wind him up and they don't like him because he's not into drugs. He did become violent on one occasion when a member of staff was accusing him of taking another boy's money. The boy had lost £20 and Charlie had just been given £20 by his Mum when he had last seen her, although he had not said anything to the staff. The missing £20 eventually turned up in the boy's room.

Being positively objective. Case sheet 1B, Children and young people: Charlie Harris

Version B

Charles Harris is a fifteen year-old boy who has been in the care of Social Services since the age of eight, when his mother became unable to look after him as a consequence of her drug addiction. During that time he has had two foster placements, each lasting less than a year before they broke down, due to Charles's disruptive and aggressive behaviour.

Charles has been regularly truanting from school during the last twelve months and has had a formal warning from the police for shop-lifting. He has also been caught joy-riding with friends on one occasion in the last two months.

Charles is moody and prone to aggressive outbursts, when he sometimes becomes violent. During one incident he threatened a member of staff with a knife. He is argumentative and is generally unpopular with the other young residents in the home. He spends most of his time with his mates on the streets and frequently stays out all night, and when he returns, he invariably smells of drink.

Being positively objective. Case sheet 1C, Learning disabilities: Mary Saunders

Version A

Mary Saunders is a twenty eight year-old Black Caribbean woman who came to this country aged four, with her parents. She has two brothers and one sister. Mary spent two years at a primary school in north London, before she was assessed as requiring special schooling. By that time she had developed many behavioural problems. Mary's mother became ill with a chronic heart condition and eventually her parents were unable to cope with Mary. At the age of fourteen she was moved into residential care.

Mary has lived in a small supported unit with three other residents for five years. The group has remained stable during that time and Mary gets on reasonably well with the others, allowing for the inevitable tensions in any group living situation. She used to attend a sheltered printing workshop where she worked with fifteen other people with learning disabilities. She was happy at the workshop where she had a number of friends. Mary was very upset when it closed down and she was moved to a local resource centre. She has lost contact with many of the people she knew at the workshop.

Mary is an energetic and sociable young woman, although she can be prone to unpredictable mood swings and has quite a temper when she feels frustrated. She likes to be part of a group and will often take the initiative in social activities. Although she was popular in the more structured environment of the workshop, she has found it difficult to settle at the resource centre, where some members have complained about her 'bossiness' and her outbursts of temper. Mary has found the more open and flexible setting of the centre hard to adjust to. Mary likes a secure routine and feels anxious without it. She has become very unhappy and feels that people have 'just got it in for her', and says she does not want to remain at the centre where she thinks no one likes her.

Being positively objective. Case sheet 1C, Learning disabilities: Mary Saunders

Version B

Mary Saunders is a twenty eight year-old Black Caribbean woman with learning difficulties who was placed at the age of fourteen in the care of social services after her parents were no longer able to cope with her behavioural problems.

Mary has lived in a supported residential unit with three others for five years. Mary is regarded as a dominant figure within the household and there have been regular arguments over domestic issues. She now attends a resource centre after the closure of the sheltered printing workshop, where she previously worked.

Mary's volatile temper, and at times domineering approach, have made relationships difficult. The more controlled environment of the workshop curbed these aggressive impulses. Since moving to the resource centre, Mary's behaviour is causing increasing problems and making her unpopular with the other members. People are frightened of her. Mary is becoming more hostile and unwilling to co-operate with any attempts to integrate her into the centre.

Being positively objective. Case sheet 1D, Physical disability: Trevor Hutton

Version A

Trevor Hutton is a forty five year-old man, who developed multiple sclerosis ten years ago. He continued to work full-time as a credit controller for four years after his diagnosis. He was by this time dependent on a wheelchair except for very restricted movement in his home, where he used two sticks. His eyesight was also affected making it impossible for him to continue using a computer screen. He also suffered from regular bouts of fatigue.

Trevor was married with two children, but six months after he took medical retirement, his wife left him for someone she had been seeing for the previous two years, unknown to Trevor. She took the children with her because, as she said, Trevor would not be able to cope with them. Trevor remains very angry about the divorce and upset that he now sees his children only very occasionally, at birthdays and Christmas.

Trevor used to attend events organised by the local branch of the MS Society and joined in with fund-raising events. He made new friends and his social life revolved around branch activities. However, as Trevor's condition has continued to deteriorate, he spends more and more time at home, rarely going out. He now has difficulty speaking and finds exhausting the effort of trying to make himself understood. He is doubly incontinent which he has found very difficult to come to terms with, and feels deeply humiliated by his inability to look after himself. He has gained five stone since becoming dependent on the wheelchair and feels there is little point in bothering about his weight, as he sees no future for himself, and he no longer cares what he looks like. He has become very depressed in the last twelve months and has twice spoken to one home carer of wanting to end his life. He does not want anti-depressants as he feels he takes enough medication for the MS, and he doesn't want any more problems with side effects. He continues to relate well to both home carers who regularly attend him. He feels that they understand him and his need to express his feelings. He becomes anxious, however, when relief carers are allocated due to holidays and sickness.

Being positively objective. Case sheet 1D, Physical disability: Trevor Hutton

Version B

Mr Hutton is a forty five year-old MS sufferer of ten years. He took medical retirement six years ago. He is divorced with two children, with whom he has occasional contact.

Mr Hutton has been confined to a wheelchair for six years, has poor eyesight, speech problems and is doubly incontinent. He relies on home care support for all personal care. Mr Hutton is considerably overweight and has been unwilling to make any attempt to reduce his weight.

Mr Hutton discourages social contact, and remains a very isolated figure. He has become increasingly depressed, threatening suicide on more than one occasion, but has refused medication. He has two regular home carers, but is very resistant to anyone else going in to provide relief cover. Mr Hutton can be a very difficult man, prone to irritable moods and outbursts of temper. He resents his reliance on health and social service professionals and has been very unco-operative and demanding when discussing his needs.

Being positively objective. Case sheet 1E, Mental health: Mehmet Erman

Version A

Mehmet Erman, aged 23, came to England from Turkey, with his parents and two sisters, ten years ago, after his uncle had been arrested because of his political activities. His uncle had been living with the family and Mehmet's father, a teacher, had provided refuge for a number of individuals on the run from the police for political protest. He believed after his brother was arrested, that he and his family would be next, and so sought political asylum in this country. Asylum was finally granted eight years ago. Since then the family have been living in north London with relatives.

Mehmet found it difficult to settle in school and made slow progress with learning English. As a consequence he left school with no qualifications. He helped out in his cousin's restaurant for a year after leaving school, but when the family discovered he was gay, he lost his job and was ordered to leave the family home by his father, who is a strict Muslim. He has only had limited contact with his mother and sisters since then.

Mehmet lived rough and gradually drifted into the drugs scene, earning money as a rent boy. He formed a relationship with Peter, an older man, three years ago and moved in with him. Mehmet has been trying to give up the drugs with his partner's support, but has become increasingly depressed at his failure to become drug free. He sought help eighteen months ago but has returned to the drugs after each of his two periods of residential treatment. In that time the depression has become more severe. Four months ago his partner was diagnosed with a brain tumour which is inoperable. Mehmet made a suicide attempt two weeks ago.

Mehmet feels guilty for being unable to support his partner and for causing him so many problems. He is deeply attached to Peter and is terrified of losing him, and yet Mehmet still feels ashamed of his own homosexuality, believing it is fundamentally wrong, and that he and Peter are being punished for their unnatural feelings. Mehmet is convinced that his homosexuality is the root of all his problems, and that is why he is a failure and is no good to anyone. He believes his father was right to banish him from the family and is convinced he has broken his mother's heart.

Being positively objective. Case sheet 1E, Mental health: Mehmet Erman

Version B

Mehmet Erman is a 23 year-old Turkish man who has lived in this country for ten years after coming here with his family. Mehmet did not settle well into school and failed to gain any qualifications. He had to leave home because of his family's disapproval of his homosexuality. He then lived rough as a rent boy and became dependent on drugs.

He moved in with an older gay man three years ago and despite several attempts at treatment, is still dependent on drugs and also suffering from depression. His partner is now terminally ill and Mehmet, unable to cope with the situation, has attempted suicide. Mehmet has failed to come to terms with his homosexuality and blames it for all his problems.

Section 4: Recording Systems

Introduction

The objective of this section is to consider the importance of accessible, effective recording systems which avoid unnecessary duplication. This section includes three modules, one of which is an information presentation and two are exercises:

- The four columns evaluation: an exercise.
- Principles of effective recording systems: a presentation for information.
- Where does the information go?: an exercise.

Training module: The four columns evaluation

↗ Objective

The aim of this exercise is to encourage learners to identify and evaluate their own systems of recording, what purpose they serve, who uses them, and what would be the consequences of those systems not working effectively.

🕐 Timing

Allow 45 minutes for this exercise.

✏ Materials

You will need:

- exercise sheet: 1 (optional), *The four columns evaluation* (alternatively, groups may prefer to use paper and pens and draw their own)
- flipchart paper
- marker pens
- bluetack

ⓘ Trainer's guidelines

Step 1: allow 5 minutes

Divide the participants into small groups of three or four and explain the exercise. Each group should use a form, either exercise sheet 1 provided below, or they may prefer to do their own. The form here has vertical lines, simply for convenience, but some groups do prefer the 'columns' to be horizontal 'boxes'.

In Column 1, participants are asked to list all the different documents, forms or types of paper work in which they have to record information. In column 2, participants identify the different people who read the records, including those both internal and external to the organisation. In Column 3, participants state the reason or purpose of the record, and why it is written. In Column 4, participants list the consequences of the record not being written, or read, or being written so poorly that it is ineffective for its purpose.

Step 2: allow 25 minutes

Participants work in their groups, completing the four columns evaluation.

Step 3: allow 15 minutes

Each group feeds back by displaying their completed four columns evaluation. The trainer needs to identify from the evaluations, general issues which are agreed by all groups, and to explore any differences or inconsistencies.

Step 4: allow 15–30 minutes

This is an optional step, and is only appropriate with participants working to the same systems. Ask groups to review their systems, and to identify any unnecessary duplication, or overlap, between different recording systems. Each group is then asked to share the main points of their small group discussion with the larger group.

✓ Exercise 1: The four columns evaluation

1. Documents, records, forms	2. Who reads the record?	3. Purpose of the record	4. Consequences of the record not being written, or read, or being poorly written

Training module: Principles of effective recording systems

↗ Objective

The aim of this module is to identify the principles of effective recording systems.

🕐 Timing

Allow 5 minutes for this module.

Materials

You will need:

- overhead projector (OHP)
- overhead transparencies:
  - OHT2 *The purpose of recording systems*
  - OHT3 *Recording systems*
    (alternatively the information can be presented on the flipchart)

ⓘ Trainer's guidelines

Step 1: allow 5 minutes

The trainer presents the two principles set out on *Recording systems,* OHT2 and OHT3, and invites responses from the participants in the form of questions, and discussion of the different points.

Recording systems should be:

Efficient and Effective

in the

Recording and Retrieval

of

Information

Recording systems should:

Be Accessible

simple to use and clear about
where the information is recorded

Be Precise in their Purpose

record only the information required
for the purpose of providing the service

Avoid Unnecessary Duplication

save worker time in not recording the
same information more than once

Observe Confidentiality

ensure information is not shared
inappropriately

Training module: Where does the information go?

 Objective

The aim of this module is to identify where information is recorded. Learners are presented with a wide variety of pieces of information, and are asked to identify where those records would be made in their own systems.

Timing

Allow 25 minutes for this exercise.

Materials

You will need:

- Exercise sheet *Where does the information go?*
  - 2A is for groups working with older people
  - 2B is for groups working with children.
- pens

Trainer's guidelines

Step 1: allow 5 minutes

Introduce the exercise and then divide the participants into groups of three or four. Give each group a copy of the appropriate exercise sheet, and ask each group to discuss where each item of information on the sheet, would be recorded in their own systems.

Step 2: allow 10 minutes

Each group works through the appropriate exercise.

Step 3: allow 10 minutes

The trainer takes each item of information from the sheet in turn, and asks groups where they would record it. Where there are differences between participants, discuss what they are, and why and how they arise. Review the discussion in terms of the principles of good recording systems. Is information being recorded without unnecessary duplication? Is confidentiality being respected?

✓ **Exercise 2, Older people: where does the information go?**

Piece of information	Where does it go?
1. Social worker phoned about Mrs Jones, she has a hospital appointment on Tuesday at 11.30 a.m.	
2. Fire Officer called in; he's thinking of doing a review of existing facilities and wants to know when we last had a drill.	
3. Mrs Jackson had to be taken to hospital because she was in the kitchen and picked up a sharp knife. When told to put it down, she did so but cut her hand badly. She was still there at the end of shift, so I have told A&E to ring us when she's ready.	
4. Mrs Rowles bathed this evening.	
5. Incontinence pads now arrived: they are in upstairs cupboard.	
6. Mrs Riley and Miss Powell would like to have their hair permed on Monday.	
7. The cooker in Unit 1 has now been repaired and is safe to use.	
8. Mrs O'Brien's daughter will be calling tomorrow to collect her mother's glasses that she mislaid here last week. They are in a white envelope on the filing cabinet.	
9. Mrs Page's prescription may be collected from the Health Centre tomorrow morning.	

10. Miss Elliot was wandering last night, and I found her in Mr Hewitt's room.	
11. Mrs Brown has reported that her watch has gone missing from her room.	
12. Mrs Such has requested that she move to a different wing from Miss Elliott.	
13. Mr Grimes has asked for a copy of *The Times* newspaper each day during his stay with us.	
14. Please do not put woollen jumpers in the tumble dryer as they shrink.	

For the Record

✓ Exercise 3, Children and young people: where does the information go?

Piece of information	Where does it go?
1. Social worker phoned today about Kim Frost. She has arranged a visit to prospective foster carers, Mr and Mrs George on Friday 15th January at 5.00 p.m.	
2. Fire officer called in; he's thinking of doing a review of existing facilities and wants to know when we had our last drill.	
3.Trudi Noble had to be taken to hospital after she cut her finger in the kitchen while helping to prepare lunch. She was escorted by Chris Long, who has just phoned to say that Trudi will not be seen for another hour and can anyone relieve her at the hospital, as she is supposed to finish her shift in half an hour and has to get back to pick her kids up from school.	
4. Ivan Lee has had his eyebrow pierced today. He says it is too painful to touch and refuses to have it bathed. It appears very red and may be infected.	
5. We only have one packet of toilet rolls left.	
6. David Webb and Andrew Morris want to go swimming on Saturday and will need a member of staff to accompany them.	
7.The cooker has now been repaired and is safe to use.	

8. Jack Pound's sister will be calling tomorrow to collect the CD she left here last time she visited. As Jack will be out he has asked staff to give it to her. It is on the filing cabinet.	
9. Georgina Parish's prescription can be picked up at the Health Centre tomorrow morning.	
10. Debbie Griffin (young person) found Frances Hall (young person) sleep-walking last night when she got up to use the toilet. Frances does not remember anything.	
11. Liam Nelson has reported that his watch has gone missing from his room.	
12. Imogen Easter has complained about Robert Bales (young person) coming into her room without knocking.	
13. Amanda White would like Muesli for breakfast. Can it be added to this week's shopping list, please?	
14. Please do not put woollen jumpers in the tumble dryer as they shrink.	

Section 5: Guidelines on Good Practice and the Legal Framework

Introduction

The objective of this section is to provide information and advice on:

- The main purposes of recording in social care.
- How to write effective records in line with current legislation.
- Good practice in recording, with reference to the principles of plain language.

The modules identify the importance of recording and the principles of good recording practice. They rely principally on information giving topics, with some exercises designed to apply those principles. The case material in the Training Modules: *A day in the life of ...* and *The daily log* provide further opportunities for learners working in direct care provision, to apply the learning from this section.

The material is presented in the form of OHTs and handouts. All information designed for the overhead projector can be presented on the flipchart, if a projector is not available.

This section provides information on the following topics:

- Why do we record?
- The general principles of recording.
- What should be recorded?
- Guidelines for recording.
- Exercise on guidelines in effective recording, using case material.
- Confidentiality.
- The right of access to information.
- Plain English.
- Information which legislation requires to be held by a residential child care unit, and what the file record should include. Clearly this is specific to those working with children and young people.

The Trainer's guidelines assume that the first three topics in this list are presented as one module, and that the next four topics are delivered together, as another module, although the topics could be delivered individually, or presented in different combinations to suit the needs of particular learner groups. Topics which are optional, or specific to those working with children and young people, are separately identified. The timing for the information-giving topics is quite generous and assumes a degree of discussion of the points with the group.

Training module: Why, what, and how, do we record?

⬈ Objective

The aim of this module is to identify the main purposes of recording in social care, the general principles of recording and what information should be recorded.

🕐 Timing

Allow 20 minutes for this module.

✎ Materials

You will need:

- overhead projector (OHP)
- overhead transparencies:
  - OHT4: *Why record?*
  - OHT5: *General principles of recording*
  - OHT6: *What should be recorded?*
  - OHT7: *How should you record?*
- handouts:
  - HO2: *Why record?*
  - HO3: *What should be recorded?*

Alternatively the information can be presented on a flipchart.

ⓘ Trainer's guidelines

Step 1: allow 10 minutes

The trainer presents the OHT4, *Why record?* and invites responses from the participants in the form of questions or discussion of different points. They then need to give out the accompanying handout, HO2 *Why record?*

Step 2: allow 5 minutes

The trainer presents the OHT5, *General principles of recording.* You will need to allow for discussion of the points, especially the first. Explore how far participants still feel that recording, doing the paperwork, gets in the way of the 'real job', i.e. caring for people. You may wish to photocopy OHT5, and give it as a handout, in addition to using it as an acetate.

Step 3: allow 5 minutes

The trainer presents the OHT6, *What should be recorded?* and OHT7, *How should you record?* You should emphasise that different organisations and agencies will have different systems for recording, and the social services model, upon which this is based, may be adapted to suit varying circumstances and needs, although it remains a basic format. The accompanying handout, HO3, *What should be recorded?* should also be given out.

1. Accountability:

- To provide a contemporary, permanent record for future reference, which can be used as evidence in legal proceedings, internal or independent investigations, SSI and auditors' inspections.
- To fulfil legal or registration requirements:
  - statutory aspects of social care work e.g. childcare and mental health
  - health and safety
  - Data Protection Act 1998.
- To provide information to service users.

2. As part of the care process:

- To provide a useful *communication* tool between care workers and other appropriate people.
- To provide the whole care team with updated *information* about a service user's needs.
- To help the care team plan their work and ensure *continuity* of care.

▣ HO2: Why record?

1. Accountability:

- To provide a contemporary, permanent record for future reference, which can be used as evidence in legal proceedings, internal or independent investigations, SSI and auditors' inspections.
- To fulfil legal or registration requirements:
  - statutory aspects of social care work e.g. childcare and mental health
  - health and safety
  - Data Protection Act 1998
- To provide information to service users.

2. As part of the care process:

- To provide a useful *communication* tool between care workers and other appropriate people.
- To provide the whole care team with updated *information* about a service user's needs.
- To help the care team plan their work and ensure *continuity* of care.

- Record keeping is an integral part, and not a distraction from, effective and efficient delivery of quality care.
- All information recorded should be relevant to the agency's role, or potential role, in the case and should be accurate, complete, clear and up to date.
- The record demonstrates that the practitioner's duty of care has been fulfilled.

Service users should be:

- Encouraged to contribute to, and check the accuracy of, file recording.
- Informed, whenever possible, of information held about them and when it is being given to others.
- Advised of their right of access.
- Confidentiality should be observed.
- Records should be kept in a secure place.

- Service user details

- All events and contacts, relevant to the agency's role

- Assessments of need and risk

- The care plan developed to meet those needs

- Financial assessment

- Monitoring and review

- Complaints and suggestions

Special attention should be given to information relating to:

- involvement of other agencies

- wishes of service users

- opinions and observations of workers with reference to legislation, policy and best practice

- information shared with third party

- records shared with service user

- how and why decisions were made

- disagreements

HO3: What should be recorded?

1. **Service user details**

   - Names, addresses, dates of birth etc. in order to identify the service user, their carers and other appropriate contacts.
   - Information regarding health, dietary preferences, language, religion and cultural identity etc.

2. **All events and contacts**

   Particularly those:
   - relating to the case
   - relevant to the care plan
   - relevant to the agency's role or potential role
   - which includes the initial contact or referral and those involved in the case.

3. **Assessments of need and risk**

   - The assessed needs of service users and carers.
   - Whether a service user is at risk of harm from themselves or others, or is a danger to others.

4. **The care plan developed to meet those needs**
   The aims, objectives, duration and types of services planned or provided, in order to monitor their progress and effectiveness for the individual service user or carer.

5. **Financial assessment**
   The costs, charges and benefits relating to services provided.

6. **Monitoring and review**
   The intended, and actual, outcomes of service provision.

7. **Complaints and suggestions**
   Who is making the complaint, when and why, and the response.

8. Special attention should be given to information relating to:

   - The involvement of other agencies.
   - The wishes and feelings of service users and their carers and families.
   - The opinions and observations of those working with the service user with reference to legislation, policy, procedure and best practice.
   - What information is shared with another agency or individual, with appropriate dates.
   - What records have been shown or copied to service users and their carers and family.
   - How and why agency decisions have been made, and by whom, and when.
   - Any disagreements between parties and how these have been resolved.

Training module: Recording guidelines, confidentiality, and the right to access

Objective

The aim of this module is to provide advice on how to write effective records in line with current legislation and good practice in recording, and to raise awareness of the issues around confidentiality and the right to access.

Timing

Allow 40 minutes for this module.

Materials

You will need:

- handouts:
  - HO4: *Recording guidelines*
  - HO5: *Confidentiality*
  - HO6: *Right of access*
- exercise sheets:
  - 4A: Visit to Mrs Megan Llewellyn
  - 4B: Suggested record for visit to Mrs Megan Llewellyn
- pens
- paper
- overhead projector (OHP)
- overhead transparencies:
  - OHT8: *Recording guidelines*
  - OHT9: *Confidentiality*
  - OHT10: *Right of access*
- a flipchart

Trainer's guidelines

Step 1: allow 15 minutes

The trainer presents the *Recording guidelines* on OHT8 on the overhead projector. You need to emphasise that point 1 of the guidelines 'Be clear about the purpose of the record' is crucial to everything else. Once you are clear about the purpose of the record, then judgements about detail become easier to make. point 3, 'Distinguish facts from opinion', will take a little time to discuss. Explain also that points 9 and 10, 'signing records' and 'confidentiality', will be discussed in more detail later in this module. Next, give out handout, HO4, *Recording guidelines*.

Step 2: allow 5 minutes

Divide participants into groups of three or four and give out exercise sheet 4A: *Visit to Mrs Megan Llewellyn*. Ask participants to read through this, and then discuss together how they can write a more effective record of this visit, and in so doing reduce the length of the record by a third. Explain that the exercise has little to do with writing style, but everything to do with Point 1 of the guidelines, i.e. being clear about the purpose of the record.

Step 3: allow 5 minutes

take feedback from the groups and distribute exercise sheet 4b: *suggested record for visit to Mrs Megan Llewellyn*. Highlight the importance of being clear about the purpose of the record and who is, or was the service user, i.e. it is not necessarily a record of everything that happened, only what is relevant to the involvement of the agency.

Step 4: allow 7 minutes

Present the overhead transparency, OHT9, on *Confidentiality*. It may be helpful to give out the accompanying handout, HO5, *Confidentiality,* as you go through the points, so that participants can focus on the detail. If there is time, discuss how the guidelines may apply in the practical work situation of the participants.

Step 5: allow 7 minutes

Present the overhead transparency, OHT10, on *Right of access*. Again, it may be helpful to give out the accompanying handout, HO6, *Right of access*, as you go through the points, so that participants can focus on the detail. If there is time, ask participants about their experience of dealing with third party information, and the problems it has presented.

1. Be clear about the purpose of the record.

2. Know where you are going to record it.

3. Distinguish facts from opinion:
   (a) verifiable factual information
   (b) direct observations
   (d) understandings
   (e) hearsay
   (f) opinions, judgements, assessments, evaluations and recommendations

4. Remember to be *accurate*, *relevant* and *concise* while still providing a *complete* record.

5. Be clear what you are going to write about.

6. Write legibly in ink. Do not use correction fluid.

7. Use clear and unambiguous language.

8. Use language that is respectful, avoids stereotypical descriptions and values difference.

9. Sign and date each piece of recorded information, including messages.

10. Be aware of confidentiality.

11. Indicate who or where the information has come from.

12. Check the accuracy of the record with the service user if appropriate.

HO4: Recording guidelines

1. **Be clear about the purpose of the record**
   Why are you writing the record? The purpose of the record will determine
   what you write and how much detail is necessary.

2. **Know where you are going to record it**
   Be clear about the systems in which you record and where different
   information should be recorded.

3. **Distinguish facts from opinion**

   - *Verifiable factual information,* e.g. date of birth.
   - *Direct observations* by the worker, although descriptions of direct
     observation may be subject to interpretation.
   - *Understandings* are statements about how things appear, assumed to
     be true but should not be considered as facts e.g. 'it appears that' 'I
     understand that'.
   - *Hearsay* is an account given by someone else and is therefore
     unsubstantiated, second-hand information and should not be considered
     as fact. The source of the information should be clearly identified.
   - *Opinions, judgements, assessments evaluations and recommendations*
     may be based on a collective view, a considered review by the worker or
     agreed with the service user. This forms an important part of social care
     work, although the basis and reason for the opinion should also be
     stated with reference to supporting information.

4. **Remember to be accurate, relevant and concise while still providing a
   complete record**. These principles are in tension with each other, and every
   record will involve a judgement as to what information needs to be included,
   based on a clear understanding of the purpose of the record.

5. **Be clear what you are going to write about**
   As with any writing, it is useful to spend a little time planning what you want
   to say, and how you should organise the information, in order to make it
   more understandable for the reader.

6. **Write legibly in ink. Do not use correction fluid**

   The record is for other people to read and so there is little point in making
   it, if no one is able to read it. If hand-writing is a problem, then type or print.
   Records provide important evidence of what happened and what was done,
   and so any alterations should be clearly identified. Put a line through
   mistakes.

HO4: Recording guidelines (cont.)

7. Use clear and unambiguous language

- Use language that will be understood by those reading the record. Complex phrases and terminology should be avoided unless they are clearly explained.
- Avoid jargon and slang terms as their meaning may be misunderstood and can change over time.
- Identify the full name and role of all individuals.

8. Use language that is respectful, avoids stereotypical descriptions and values difference

It is important to write about individuals in respectful terms while still providing a factual record. Avoid stereotypical descriptions which reinforce discriminatory attitudes.

9. Sign and date each piece of recorded information, including messages

Full signatures are required rather than initials. Where two workers have contributed to the record they should both sign.

In some circumstances it may be important to record the time the record was made. Descriptions of an incident that were written 30 minutes or 5 hours later may view it somewhat differently.

10. Be aware of confidentiality

This relates to how information is used and where it is stored.

11. Indicate who or where the information has come from

This is particularly important in relation to third party information and may have implications for what information can be shared with the service user.

12. Check the accuracy of the record with the service user, if appropriate

Where possible service users should be involved in the process of recording.

✓ Exercise 4A: Visit to Mrs Megan Llewellyn

I visited Mrs Megan Llewellyn on 23rd October, following the death two weeks ago of her mother Nesta Morgan, who was a resident in Lovegrove House. I arranged with Mrs Llewellyn to call on Wednesday afternoon, as this is the only time through the week when she is not working. Despite her mother's death, she is concerned not to take any more time off work than necessary, as she feels her job is not very secure.

I arrived at 3.00 p.m. Mrs Llewellyn appeared very tired and said she had just had a lie down after coming in from work at lunch-time. She has not been sleeping very well and has found all the arrangements very difficult. She said that the funeral is causing problems, in that there are members of the family who have been estranged for many years and resent each other attending. I said that Freda Hall, Mrs Morgan's keyworker would like to attend the funeral, if that was alright. Mrs Llewellyn said she would welcome anyone coming from the home including the other residents. She said that she thought Kathleen Sykes and Ruth Baxter, who were her mother's special friends, would be coming.

She said how kind everyone had been. She felt her mother's last years had been very happy ones because of the care she received at Lovegrove House. The staff had been especially thoughtful when her mother died, and she would like to show her appreciation in some way. She thought she would make a donation to the home.

I explained that I had brought the remainder of her mother's things. Mrs Llewellyn apologised for the trouble she had put the staff to, but she couldn't face going through her mother's clothes and possessions. She wanted the clothes given to a charity shop and the rest returned to her. I explained that the clothes had been given to 'Help the Aged', that a list had been drawn up of the rest of her mother's possessions, and asked if she would like to check them. Mrs Llewellyn became upset while going through the list but agreed that everything was there and signed that she had received them. Mrs Llewellyn said there was nothing of any real value but some things were of great sentimental value, and her mother had indicated who she wanted certain things passed on to, although she had never made a will.

Mrs Llewellyn said she found it hard being the only child. There were no brothers or sisters to turn to and she had lost her own husband five years ago with a heart attack. Her father died fifteen years ago from cancer. She felt very alone, although she said she had friends who were being very supportive and she enjoyed good health, so she counted herself quite fortunate.

Mrs Llewellyn said that she thought she would feel better when the funeral was over. It was the day after tomorrow and although it would be very emotional, she felt it was important to say goodbye properly. She wanted flowers and music and had planned the service with the vicar. She wanted it to be a day for remembering her mother and she just hoped the rest of the family would not spoil it. I reassured her that families usually rise to the occasion and put aside their differences in such circumstances. Mrs Llewellyn again thanked the department for all their support.

✓ Exercise 4B: Suggested record for visit to Mrs Megan Llewellyn

Worker: Leslie Rudge
Purpose of Visit: To return possessions of the late Mrs Morgan, resident of Lovegrove House, to her daughter Mrs Megan Llewellyn
Date: 23rd October, 2000

Following the death of Mrs Nesta Morgan, her daughter Mrs Llewellyn indicated that she did not feel able to sort through her mother's possessions and wished staff at Lovegrove House to give her mother's clothes to charity and return the rest to her. Mrs Llewellyn became upset while checking through the list, but agreed that everything was there and signed that she had received the items listed.

Mrs Morgan's funeral will be held on Friday 25th October. I indicated that Freda Hall, Mrs Morgan's Keyworker, would like to attend. Mrs Llewellyn said that members of staff and residents from Lovegrove House would be welcome and that she understood that Kathleen Sykes and Ruth Baxter, residents, who were her mother's special friends, were coming.

Mrs Llewellyn expressed her appreciation for all the kindness that the staff at Lovegrove House had shown her mother and thanked the department for all their support.

1. Personal information

2. 'Need to know'

3. One purpose

4. Disclosure without consent:
   - protection
   - crime
   - legal requirement

5. Informing service users

6. Maintaining security:
   - storage
   - transferring information
   - discussions
   - third parties

7. Case Files, communication books and diaries

8. Information about other service users

HO5: Confidentiality

1. Personal information

All information about a service user should be considered as confidential. Personal information should normally be available only to staff working directly with the service user.

2. 'Need to know'

Others who may 'need to know' include:

- social work finance staff as part of financial assessments
- legal advisers, when actual or possible court proceedings arise
- other agencies who may be working with, or on behalf of, local authorities
- supervisors and managers
- social work students, practice teachers and tutors when undertaking direct work with service users

3. One purpose

Information supplied for one purpose should not be used for another purpose.

4. Disclosure without consent

Information may need to be disclosed without the consent of the service user, but only if sanctioned by a team or unit manager in order to:

- protect children, individuals or the public, including risks to public health based on medical advice
- help to prevent, detect or prosecute a serious crime
- meet legal requirements, e.g. subpoena

5. Informing service users

Service users should be informed when information has been disclosed about them, unless there are good reasons not to inform, and it is agreed with the team or unit manager. However, seeking permission in advance of information being shared, should be considered best practice.

6. Maintaining security

In order to ensure that information is not disclosed unintentionally:

- all recorded information should be stored securely
- when information is being transferred, care should be taken to ensure that it arrives at its intended destination and is not accessed en route, e.g. marked 'confidential', secure e-mails.
- discussions about service users should only take place where they cannot be overheard by members of the public or other service users
- information is never given to a third party without checking their identity

 **HO5: Confidentiality** (cont.)

7. **Case files**

Personal information relating to the individual service user should be recorded on their case file and not in general communication books or diaries. It is enough that a reference is made in these general communication systems, directing the reader to the case file for further information.

8. **Information about other service users**

Information about a service user should not be recorded in any case file other than their own. Where an incident may involve two or more service users, only a minimal reference, necessary to make the information meaningful, should be made to any service users, other than the individual service user whose case file it is.

1. **Data Protection Act 1998**

- incorporates:
  - Access to Personal Files Act 1987
  - Access to Health Records Act 1990
- encourages a more open and sharing way of working with service users

2. **Restricted access**

- prevention or detection of crime
- risk of serious harm to service user or prejudice social work
- third party consent
- information restricted by statute

3. **Rights of access for under 18s and advocates**

- requests by, or on behalf of under 18s
- requests made on behalf of an adult lacking mental capacity
- requests made through an agent
- deceased persons

4. **Third party information**

- third party veto can no longer be assumed

▣ HO6: Right of access

1. Data Protection Act 1998

The right of access to information is now determined by the most recent Data Protection Act 1998 (DPA) which came into force on 31st March 2000. It incorporates the Access to Personal Files Act 1987 and the Access to Health Records Act 1990.

The Access to Personal Files Act 1987 encouraged a more open and sharing way of working with service users.

All information whether on manual or computer records is subject to the new DPA.

The DPA requires that personal data shall be:

- adequate, relevant and not excessive
- accurate and where necessary kept up to date
- not kept for longer than is necessary for its purpose

Service users have a right of access to the information held about them, which includes:

- factual information
- expressions of opinion
- the intentions of the authority in relation to their case

Where access is refused, service users may appeal to the courts or the Data Protection Commissioner.

2. Restricted access

Information may still be restricted where:

1. Disclosure may interfere with the prevention or detection of crime.
2. Disclosure will prejudice social work or cause serious harm to the physical or mental health of the service user.
3. Disclosure of physical or mental health information cannot be made without consulting an 'appropriate health professional'.
4. Information is restricted by statute, e.g. adoption records, parental order records, section 30 of the Human Fertilisation and Embryology Act 1990.

HO6: Right of access (cont.)

3. Rights of access for children and young people under 18 and advocates

The following may be permitted:

1. *Requests by, or on behalf of, a child or young person under 18.* The local authority must believe that the young person understands what it means to exercise their right of access.
2. *Requests made on behalf of an adult lacking mental capacity.* If a service user lacks capacity to manage their affairs, a person acting under the Court of Protection or within the terms of a registered Enduring Power of Attorney can request access on their behalf.
3. *Requests made through another person (an Agent).* If a service user has the mental capacity and if they have appointed an agent, that agent can request access on behalf of the service user.
4. *Requests for access to the records of a deceased person.* The Data Protection Act applies only to data about those still living.

4. Third party information

A third party is anyone not employed by the local authority holding the records.

Under the Access to Personal Files Act 1987, third party information would not be shared with the service user without the express permission of the third party who had supplied the information.

With the new Data Protection Act, the status of third party information appears to have changed in as much as the third party veto can no longer be assumed. It would seem that third party information can be shared unless the third party has stated otherwise.

Depending on the circumstances, the service user may be told the nature of the information but not the source.

It may be necessary to discuss with third parties the value of sharing information with the service user, and recognise the poor practice of withholding information because it is considered 'upsetting' or 'awkward'.

Training module: 'Plain English'

 Objective

The aim of this module is to introduce, and to explore, the principles of 'Plain English'.

Timing

Allow 30 minutes for this module.

Materials

You will need:

- exercise sheets:
  - 5A: 'Plain English' questionnaire
  - 5B: 'Plain English' answers
- paper
- pens
- handout HO7: *'Plain English'*

Trainer's guidelines

Step 1: allow 10 minutes

Give out the exercise sheet 5A: *'Plain English' questionnaire* and ask participants to complete it. (The *Questionnaire* and the *Answers Sheet* below, are adapted from *Plain English for Social Services* by Graham Hopkins, 1998.)

Step 2: allow 10 minutes

Give out the exercise sheet 5B: *'Plain English' answers* with the suggested answers. Discuss the answers with the group.

Step 3: allow 10 minutes

Give out the handout, HO7, *'Plain English'* and read through the points with the group, illustrating and discussing points.

✓ Exercise 5A: 'Plain English' questionnaire

Please rewrite the following phrases or sentences, putting them into clear, concise and effective English:

1. A sharp decrease in the number of referrals was noted.

   _____

2. References are always sought prior to commencing employment.

   _____

3. The staff are all female with the exception of one male who is the manager.

   _____

4. Placement agreements which are amended and modified on a regular basis.

   _____

5. There are tea making facilities should any resident wish to avail themselves. Not all are acceptable but some do take advantage.

   _____

6. Inspectors suggested that consideration be given to radical re-design of the grounds which are extensive and grossly underused.

   _____

7. Inspectors were informed that a separate handbook intended for parents was in the final stages of preparation.

   _____

8. The thrust of the approach to health care at this home is the preventative approach.

   _____

9. It should be ensured that all clients are made aware of their right to complain in writing.

   _____

✓ Exercise 5B: 'Plain English' answers

Your rewritten statements could look something like this:

1. A sharp decrease in the number of referrals was noted.

Referrals fell sharply.

2. References are always sought prior to commencing employment.

References will be taken up before you start working for us.

3. The staff are all female with the exception of one male who is the manager.

The staff are all female with the exception of the manager.

4. Placement agreements which are amended and modified on a regular basis

Placement agreements are amended on a regular basis.

5. There are tea making facilities should any resident wish to avail themselves. Not all are acceptable but some do take advantage.

Some residents make themselves a hot drink.

6. Inspectors suggested that consideration be given to radical re-design of the grounds which are extensive and grossly underused.

Inspectors suggested that work should be done on the large grounds as not much use is made of them at the moment.

7. Inspectors were informed that a separate handbook intended for parents was in the final stages of preparation.

A separate handbook for parents will be ready soon.

8. The thrust of the approach to health care at this home is the preventative approach.

The home takes a preventative approach to health care.

9. It should be ensured that all clients are made aware of their right to complain in writing.

All clients should be made aware in writing of their right to complain.

▣ HO7: 'Plain English'

'Plain English' is concerned with ensuring written communications use language that is simple and direct, so that it can be easily understood.

It is especially concerned with written communication in the workplace, where language should be used to communicate with, rather than impress or intimidate others.

Plain English has limited relevance to creative or literary writing, where artistic expression depends on an enriched use of language.

Guidelines for Plain English and clear writing

1. Keep sentences short and clear, ideally 15–20 words.

2. Generally use active verbs. Write 'We will introduce it' instead of 'It will be introduced'. This also clarifies responsibility for action.

3. Use short and familiar words rather than long ones. Avoid legalistic and pompous words.

4. Only use jargon if your readers will understand it.

5. Avoid ambiguous words, which are open to misinterpretation.

6. Plan how to structure and present the information with your readers in mind.

7. Keep to essentials and get to the point.

8. Use lists where appropriate to break down information into separate points.

9. Use short paragraphs, which contain one idea or concept.

10. Use punctuation to help understanding.

11. Certain traditional rules of grammar no longer apply. For instance it is acceptable to start a sentence with a conjunction, e.g. 'and', 'but', 'because'.

12. Where appropriate directly address your readers. Use 'I' and 'you'.

13. Adopt a positive tone, try to avoid sounding defensive or patronising.

14. Avoid using double negatives, e.g. 'He shouldn't be not looking when he's driving.'

15. Try to avoid using unnecessary words or expressions which do not add to the meaning of the sentence, e.g. 'Procedures have been revised and updated.'

Training module: Statutory record keeping in residential child care

 Objective

This module deals with the information which statute requires must be kept on individual children in residential care. The legislation is the Children's Homes Regulations 1991. The module also deals with what the file record should include. Clearly this module will not be appropriate for learners working with adults.

 Timing

Allow 40 minutes for this module.

Materials

You will need:

- paper
- pens
- flipchart and markers
- handout HO7: *Childrens Homes Regulations 1991*

Trainer's guidelines

Step 1: allow 10 minutes

Divide participants into groups of three or four. Ask each group to list the information they are legally required to keep.

Step 2: allow 10 minutes

Take feedback from the groups by listing information on the flipchart. Next distribute the handout, HO8, *Children's Homes Regulations 1991*, and compare what is on the flipchart with the handout. Discuss any differences.

Step 3: allow 10 minutes

Ask the participants in the same small groups to look at the handout and discuss how their own records compare. Do they keep all the information on the file record that is suggested? How effective do they consider their own file records?

Step 4: allow 10 minutes

Take feedback from the groups, and discuss the issues arising.

▣ HO8: Children's Homes Regulations 1991

Information required by statute to be kept on an individual child by a residential care unit:

1. The child's name and any name by which the child has previously been known other than a name used by the child prior to adoption.

2. The child's sex and date of birth.

3. The child's religious persuasion, if any.

4. A description of the child's racial origin, cultural and linguistic background.

5. Where the child has come from before they were accommodated in the home.

6. The person by whose authority the child is provided with care and accommodation in the home, and the statutory provision under which they are so provided.

7. The name, address and telephone number and the religious persuasion, if any of:
(a) the child's parents
(b) any person who is not a parent of the child but who has parental responsibility for them.

8. The name, address and telephone number of any social worker for the time being assigned to the child by the local authority looking after them or by the voluntary organisation or the person carrying on the registered children's home who are providing the child with accommodation.

9. The date and circumstances of any visit to the child whilst in the home by any persons referred to in Regulation 8 (2) (c).

10. A copy of any Statement of Special Educational Needs under Section 7 of the Education Act 1981 maintained in relation to the child with details of any such needs.

11. The name and address of any school or college attended by the child, and any employer of the child.

12. Every school report received by the child while accommodated in the home.

13. The date and circumstances of any disciplinary measures imposed on the child.

14. Any special dietary or health needs of the child.

15. Arrangements for, including any restrictions on, or contact between the child and:
(a) their parents
(b) any person who is not a parent but who has parental responsibility for them
(c) any other person.

HO8: Children's Homes Regulations 1991 (cont.)

16. The date and result of any review of the child's case.

17. The name and address of the medical practitioner with whom the child is registered.

18. Details of any accident involving the child.

19. Details of any immunisation, illness, allergy or medical examination or dental need of the child.

20. Details of any health examination or developmental test conducted with respect to the child at or in connection with their school.

21. Details of all medical products taken by the child while in the home and by whom they were administered, including those which the child is permitted to administer themselves.

22. The date on which any money or valuables are deposited by or on behalf of a child for safe keeping, and the date on which any valuables are returned.

23. Where the child goes to when they cease to be accommodated in the home.

Training module: A day in the life of . . .

⬈ Objective

The aim of this module is to demonstrate the importance of recording, which is both regular and relates to the objectives laid down in the careplan. The exercise is designed to help learners appreciate the need to provide a regular account of what is happening with a service user. It illustrates the limitations of an approach which only concentrates on recording 'problems', or 'unusual' occurrences, where individual service users who do not appear to have any particular problems, may be easily overlooked.

The material provides the opportunity for participants to consider how systematic recording is an essential part of effective careplanning. Once again, there are different versions, and different case sheets, for those working with different client groups. The Trainer's guidelines illustrate one version, *Henry*, and for each of the other versions, trainers should follow the same procedure, but incorporate the changes set out on the notes accompanying the relevant case sheet.

🕐 Timing

Allow 45 minutes for this module.

✏️ Materials

- case sheets, *A Day in the Life of . . .*
  - 2A: Older people. Henry
  - 2B: Children and young people. Claire
  - 2C: Learning disabilities. Brian
  - 2D: Physical disability. Surinder Birdi
  Sheets 2B, 2C, and 2D have discussion notes attached.
- flipchart
- paper
- pens

ⓘ Trainer's guidelines

Step 1: allow approximately 15 minutes

Divide the participants into small groups of two, three or four individuals. Give them a copy of the relevant case sheet for the group you are working with. Ask them to read it through individually, and then collectively to write a likely record of Henry's (or Claire's, or whichever version you are using) day. It is important to emphasise that this should be a *typical* rather than an *ideal* record, and that no careworker has been privy to Henry's thoughts, nor would be aware of Henry's actions when he has been alone. The careworker's record is therefore likely to be very limited. Participants may feel very concerned about Henry, because they, unlike the careworkers in the story, are aware of his distress and want to write what they think should be written, rather than what would normally be written. Reassure them that they will have this opportunity later on in the exercise.

Next, the groups should read aloud their records, which may include 'usual day', 'no problems', 'Henry spent quiet day, ate well', 'Henry did not attend sing-a-long', or variations on these themes.

Step 2: allow approximately 10 minutes

Participants should then be asked how adequate they feel the records are as a description of what is happening with Henry.

Participants will usually say the record is inadequate but sometimes make the point that shortage of staff and lack of time makes these very shorthand records more likely. This pressure needs to be acknowledged, but at the same time ask participants to consider how Henry's quality of care could be improved through more effective recording.

Step 3: allow approximately 10 minutes

Ask participants in their small groups to consider how Henry's careplan could be used to identify a more positive way of working with him. Participants should be encouraged to think about his likes and dislikes, his needs, and how those can be best met while still promoting his independence.

Each group is asked to share their ideas and comment on the ideas put forward by the other groups. These ideas can be written up on the flipchart.

Step 4: allow approximately 10 minutes

Finally, ask participants how they think the daily recording might contribute in monitoring the effective implementation of the careplan. It is important to emphasise how this shifts the focus from one exclusively concerned with problems to one that is also assessing progress.

A story I often share at this point, is one that was told to me by a participant whose own mother had gone into residential care. The elderly lady had initially been a quiet and unassuming individual who attracted little attention from hard pressed careworkers. After six months of being docile and co-operative, she became increasingly difficult and disruptive. The daughter believed it was her mother's reaction to being largely ignored. It would appear that the mother learnt that if you were a problem you got attention. And so careworkers may, without realising it, encourage service users to be more demanding.

If careworkers only believe there is something worthwhile to record when there is a problem, they may actually increase the incidence of those problems. With a proactive and positive approach to recording and careplanning the quality of care for service users can be improved and this helps prevent the problems from arising in the first place.

Case sheet 2A, Older people: A day in the life of Henry

Henry, aged 81, has been a resident in the home for over a year since the death of his wife. When he first arrived, he seemed quite bewildered and had been extremely withdrawn. He was often crying on his own in his room. He was not a strong man and frequently developed colds and other minor ailments, although his health was not considered a serious problem.

Henry awoke on Thursday 13th July to a grey overcast morning. He thought about his son and daughter-in-law who were on holiday in France. He remembered back to the holidays he had enjoyed with his wife. He recalled the last one before she died. They had gone to Pembroke, where they had been many times before. She loved Pembroke. They were no longer able to walk very far but they enjoyed sitting on the front at Tenby. It was such a pretty place and they had been very happy during that fortnight. The weather had been kind. That was over eleven years ago now. She had had a stroke soon after the holiday and he had nursed her at home for the last decade of her life. He looked out of the window at the garden. It was spacious and well maintained with lots of shrubs. He was fond of sitting out there when the sun shone. But there were no roses. He had always loved roses but he was told they took too much work.

He listened outside and heard footsteps along the corridor. Soon Angela knocked on the door and popped her head round. She said 'Good morning' and asked how he was feeling. He replied as he always did, 'Not too bad thank you'. Angela said she would be back in a few minutes, only she wanted to see how Mrs Andrews was, as she had apparently been rather poorly in the night. After about fifteen minutes, Angela came back and helped Henry to get washed and dressed. Henry had felt very embarrassed to begin with and was still a little uncomfortable at having to rely on others to assist him with such personal aspects of his daily routine. Angela was such a cheerful character and would always chatter on. But Henry liked to be quiet in the mornings and found the noisy bustle rather disconcerting.

When he arrived for breakfast, he tried to sit with Geoff, whom he had slowly got to know over the last few months. Geoff however, had been joined by Mary, who had recently moved to the home and was a very lively lady and had obviously taken a shine to Geoff. Henry didn't want to intrude and besides he didn't really like Mary. She was always talking about herself and her children and never seemed to give anyone else the chance to talk. Henry sat down with Albert. Albert was fairly quiet and kept himself to himself and that suited Henry. They ate their breakfast in mutual silence.

After breakfast Henry returned to his room with his daily paper and sat reading until coffee time. He was reluctant to go down to the lounge but he knew the staff did not like residents remaining in their room for too long, so he made the effort to take coffee with the others. At least the weather had brightened a little. He might even be able to go outside after lunch. When he arrived in the lounge, Angela was already serving coffee and came over with a cup as soon as he sat down. She had put a biscuit in his saucer. It was a digestive. He didn't like digestives and had said so before but no one seemed to remember. He had given up saying anything. They meant well, after all, and he knew they already thought he was a bit of a miserable old so-and-so.

Henry sat alone and gazed out of the window, not looking at anything in particular. Edith, another resident called across to him and asked if he was looking forward to the sing-song this afternoon. He said he had forgotten about it and thought he might go outside if it was warm enough. Edith said he didn't know what he was missing. It was a lot of fun and everyone had a good time singing all the old songs. Henry remembered how his wife had used to sing. She had a lovely voice and played the piano as well. He remembered how thrilled she had been when they were finally able to afford to buy a piano. They had both loved music. That was how they had met. She had been singing in the same choir as his sister and he had gone along to one of the concerts and been introduced to her.

Angela suddenly interrupted his thoughts and asked if he would be coming along to the sing-a-long. Henry repeated what he had said to Edith. He returned to his room feeling very weary. He looked at the paper again but didn't feel he wanted to do the crossword after all. Instead he switched on the radio and listened to Radio 3. They were playing his favourite composer, Mozart.

At 12.30 p.m. Fiona, another careworker, knocked on the door to remind him lunch was nearly ready. Henry was actually feeling quite hungry and looked forward to something to eat. When he entered the dining room Mary was once again already sitting with Geoff. Henry sat with Albert. He enjoyed the lamb hotpot. The apple pie was only lukewarm and the custard was too runny but he finished it nevertheless. Albert said he didn't want custard but no one heard him and they put a bowl with custard in front of him. He looked at Henry helplessly. Henry called out to Angela and said that Albert didn't want any custard. Angela looked flustered but changed the bowl for one without custard. Albert smiled gratefully at Henry.

After lunch, Henry fetched his coat and went outside to sit in the garden. It was still a little chilly and the sun continued to make only fleeting appearances between the cloud. Henry could hear the singing inside. He walked slowly to the bench further down the garden. He looked at the shrubs. They were mostly spring varieties and their blossoms had long disappeared. He thought about the roses. He had grown so many. They had won prizes at local shows. He looked across the garden and thought how much brighter it would look with some more flowers. He closed his eyes and remembered his own garden. Suddenly his peace was disturbed by the sound of the lawn mower. He looked up confused. It wasn't the usual day for cutting the grass. Colin, the part-time gardener sensed his confusion and explained that, as he was going on holiday for a fortnight, he had to tidy things up before he went.

Henry couldn't bear the noise and made his way inside. Inevitably, people thought he had come in to join in with the sing-song. He mumbled something about Colin, and the lawnmower, and escaped to his room. He sat down in his chair. He felt so lonely. Suddenly he wanted to cry. He hadn't felt like that for months. He tried to stop himself but the tears trickled down his face.

Case sheet 2B, Children and young people: A day in the life of Claire

Claire, aged fourteen, heard noises outside her room. She still felt sleepy and the room was cold. She looked toward the window. She really didn't like those curtains. The staff had told her that she could arrange the room as she wanted. But that was nearly four weeks ago, when she first arrived and no one had said anything since. Claire liked bright colours but everything in the room was dark. Navy curtains and carpet and dark blue wallpaper with that stupid pattern. Her social worker had said that she wouldn't be there that long, but she had only seen her once since she had arrived.

It was the 5th of June, her mother's birthday. Last year she had bought her Mum some perfume. She had really liked it. They were getting on well then. Her Mum had been a lot happier. Claire's Dad had walked out when she was only four. She couldn't really remember much about him and they never heard from him. Her Mum had been very depressed for a long time but seemed better after she started working at the local pub. But then she met Martin and he moved in after they had gone to Spain together for a holiday. Claire had never liked him. He always thought he knew everything and then when he started coming into her room when her Mum was out, she tried to stop him. She tried to tell her Mum but they just said she was trying to make trouble: until she got pregnant. And then her Mum accused her of sleeping around and being a slut. She had stayed out nights but that was because she didn't want to go home. And even after she'd taken the tablets and had to go to hospital, her mother still didn't want to know. She told social services she couldn't cope with Claire anymore. So Claire had an abortion and was then sent to Melrose House.

At least it was Saturday and she didn't have to go to school. She hated school. The only thing she was any good at was art, but what was the use of that. It wouldn't get her a job. She heard Sandra, one of the care staff calling to Ben, who had the room next to hers. He always had his radio on really loud. Sandra told him to turn it down. It was a bit quieter for a few minutes but then Ben turned it up once more. Claire had wanted a lie-in, but she was feeling restless and hungry by now. She pulled on some clothes, looked for her hairbrush, but couldn't find it and went down to the kitchen.

Karen and Julie were there already, making themselves some toast. Sandra had made some tea and asked Claire if she wanted any. Claire hated tea and said she would make herself some coffee. Claire looked in the cupboard. She wanted some 'Cheerios'. They had run out and she had reminded Don yesterday to get some when he went shopping, but he had obviously forgot them. She complained to Sandra, who said she would definitely put it down on the list for the next shopping trip. Claire scanned the boxes of cereals and reluctantly pulled out some 'Cornflakes'. Julie and

Karen continued to talk about some girl at school they knew, whom they obviously didn't like. Claire did not recognise the name and did not join in the conversation. Sandra had gone to answer the phone in the office. Claire quickly finished her breakfast and returned to her room.

She thought again about her mother. She wondered if they'd organise a party. Her Mum was forty and Claire supposed her Mum might want a bit of a 'do'. Her elder brother, Kevin, would enjoy that. He always liked a party. She hadn't heard anything from Kevin since she left home. Claire had sent her Mum a birthday card. She wondered if she would hear anything back, maybe a phone call or something. She thumbed through a magazine she had bought yesterday. There was a knock at the door. It was Sandra. She asked if Claire wanted to go swimming. Some of the others wanted to go. Claire said she didn't feel like it. She wanted to see something on television anyway. Sandra said that Pete, the other member of staff on duty would be around if she needed anything. Claire nodded and carried on with the magazine, which she wasn't really reading anyway.

She thought about Shirley, her brother's girlfriend. She had always liked Shirley, and Shirley had been the only one to come and visit her in hospital. She had spoken to her a few times on the phone since she had arrived at Melrose, but Shirley didn't really say much about Claire's Mum or Martin. Still Claire thought it might be an idea to give Shirley a ring. She might know what was happening for her Mum's birthday and whether she had got the card. Claire went down to the phone and dialled Shirley's number. There was no answer. She hung on for a couple of minutes but Shirley must be out. Claire looked at the clock in the hallway; it was nearly time for the programme she wanted to watch.

Claire went into the lounge and found Ben and Larry sprawled out on the sofas. They were watching something on another channel. She said she wanted to watch something else but they said that they had got there first and weren't changing the programme for her. She'd already had a few arguments with Ben and really didn't feel in the mood for one today. So she left them to it and went back to her room.

After about half an hour Pete shouted up that there was a phone call for her. Claire wondered if it might be her Mum. She ran downstairs. It was her friend Toni. She wanted Claire to come shopping with her. She had some birthday money to spend, but Claire said she didn't want to go shopping and she didn't have any money anyway. Claire went back upstairs. She didn't want to stay in her room, but she didn't want to miss her Mum if she did ring. She didn't want to talk to anyone in the house, but she felt so miserable on her own.

Pete knocked on the door and asked if she wanted to help get lunch ready. She said she was going to have a bath and wash her hair. Claire ran a really deep hot bath and locked herself in the bathroom for the next hour. She nearly fell asleep but was aroused when she heard the others *return from swimming. Julie and Karen were laughing and giggling over something, but she couldn't hear what they were saying. Sandra banged on the bathroom door and told Claire to hurry up for lunch, Pete had cooked something special.*

She went down and discovered that Pete had been making home made pizzas. They tasted alright but she couldn't see why he had bothered. Everyone gathered round the large kitchen table. Ben and Larry were arguing about something. Sandra asked Karen and Julie where the party was they were going to that evening. They weren't sure but their mate Lisa knew. Sandra asked Claire if she had any plans for the evening. Claire shrugged and said she might go out with her friend Toni. Claire helped with the washing up and then returned to her room, where she continued to wait for the phone to ring.

A day in the life of Claire: notes for discussion

Points that might be noted in the daily recording:

- Claire complaining about lack of 'Cheerios'
- not joining Sandra, Julie and Karen for swimming
- phone call
- spent an hour in the bath
- might go out in the evening with friend, Toni

Issues that need to be identified in the Careplan Objectives:

- Working on feelings about her family, especially her mother. Her mother's birthday was very significant to Claire and although care staff cannot reasonably be expected to be alert to the date of her mother's birthday, if they had been working more closely with Claire, she might have talked with them about it.
- Making Claire feel more comfortable in her room. What about the colour scheme? Why can't she be encouraged to repaint the walls and make it feel more like her own space for the time she is there?
- Discussion of long term options. Claire needs to know what is happening and when she might see her social worker again.
- Discussion of feelings about school and opportunities to develop more confidence through the activities she likes and feels she can do well, e.g. art.

Case sheet 2C, Learning disability: A day in the life of Brian

Brian awoke at 6.30 a.m. He always woke early. He didn't need an alarm clock. He was always up before anyone else in the house. He looked out of the window. It was raining. Brian liked the rain. He especially liked walking in it, but his mother would tell him that was silly. He suddenly remembered he had promised to take a tape in for Penny. She had only started at the Resource Centre a few weeks ago, but they were already good friends. Brian rummaged under his bed. He found the magazine he had been looking for, but not the tape. He decided to go to the toilet and look for the tape afterwards. As soon as Brian opened his door, Alfie the dog came running up stairs and started barking. Brian heard his Mum and Dad start to stir.

After he returned to his room, he continued looking for the tape, while Alfie ran around his room, barking more and more excitedly. Brian's Dad stuck his head round the door and told Brian to keep the dog quiet. Brian's Mum shouted to Brian to start getting ready. Brian sat and played with Alfie.

Brian was 24 years old. He had been born with Down's Syndrome and lived with his parents and his sister who was away on a school trip to France. Brian attended the Resource Centre five days a week. His father worked with the Post Office and his mother was training to be a teacher.

Brian's Mum came into his room and started sorting his clothes, putting out clean underwear, saying that the dirty set were ready to walk off by themselves. She told him to go and get washed. Brian ambled off to the bathroom. His mother reminded him to shave as he hadn't bothered yesterday. Brian's father grumbled from the landing that Brian was more lazy than anything else. Brian's Mum went down to the kitchen with his Dad. He could hear them still going on about him. He heard his father saying that his mother did too much and she was wearing herself out with the teaching as well as Brian. Brian ought to be made to do more for himself. Brian's Mum said he didn't understand, he'd never understood. Soon they were shouting at one another.

Brian struggled to put his clothes on. He didn't like it when his Mum and Dad argued. They had always had arguments, but it seemed a lot worse since she had started her course. Brian wished she still stayed at home. He pulled a comb through his hair and went downstairs.

Brian's Mum was crying. His Dad was going out of the door. His mother told him not to take any notice and put his breakfast on the table. She went upstairs to the bathroom. Brian sat and ate his breakfast. He listened to the radio but he was worried about his Mum. She came downstairs just before the bus came to take him to the Resource Centre and told him everything was alright. She did his coat up, gave him a kiss and waved him off.

Brian sat quietly for most of the journey. His friend, Martin told him about this really good film he had seen with his brother but Brian was not very interested. Martin went and sat with George. On arriving at the Centre, Brian went off to look for Penny. He had forgotten the tape but he wanted to see her. Penny would sometimes spend the mornings helping out in the kitchen, but Wendy, the cook, told Brian that Penny wasn't coming into today, her mother had phoned in to say she was ill.

Brian wandered over to the computer area. He liked playing with the games and was quite good. There were still a few machines free, so he settled down. Frank, who was the member of staff in charge, was busy with Tracey. Tracey was learning word processing and was already able to do the Centre newsletter. Brian didn't like Tracey. He thought she was too full of herself. Frank nodded at Brian and said he would be over in a minute as he had a new game Brian might like to try. Brian played patiently and didn't say anything, although he was looking forward to the new game.

Soon the room filled up and there were no more free computers. Kieran, the manager came in and said there was an important phone call for Frank. After Frank left the room, Olly came in. Olly looked around the room and walked over to Brian. Olly was big and liked to get his own way. Olly said he had some important work to get on with and Brian was just playing stupid games. Brian was afraid of Olly, especially when there were no staff around. Olly had once kicked him very hard deliberately when they were playing football. But Jake, the staff member, hadn't seen anything and Olly just sneered at Brian as he struggled to continue playing. Brian didn't say anything.

Olly told Brian to get out of the way. Brian was angry. He wanted to finish his game and he was sick of Olly pushing him around, but Olly started trying to shove him off his chair. Olly was trying to make out it was a big joke. Everyone was looking. Brian had had enough and he just got up and walked out. Olly was laughing as Brian left the room.

Brian went out into the garden. It was still raining. Fiona came out of the greenhouse and said how she had intended clearing some of the leaves as there were so many now, but it was raining and she would have to leave it. Brian said he would do it. He liked the rain and so he went and got his coat and spent the next half an hour sweeping the leaves and putting them on the compost.

Brian came in for coffee. Frank came over and asked him if he wanted to play the new game. Brian said he was bored with computers. Frank asked if Olly had said anything to him. Brian shook his head. Frank said that if Brian changed his mind, he would show him how it worked. After coffee, Brian went back outside. The rain had stopped and he spent the rest of the morning tidying up. Fiona said what a good job he'd done.

Brian was not really hungry but he ate all his lunch. His Mum told him he was getting too fat but Brian had a sweet tooth. He had two portions of pudding. After lunch Martin asked Brian if he wanted to play a game of cards. Brian agreed. Martin told him all over again about the film he'd seen with his brother, but Brian didn't mind, he was pleased to be doing something and Martin was always friendly.

Soon it was time for the bus to go home. Brian would have to stay with Harriet, the lady who lived next door, until his Mum came home. Brian sat and watched television. Harriet made him some tea and gave him a piece of cake. His mother got home later than usual, saying that she had got held up. She cooked dinner for Brian and herself, saying Dad was working late. After dinner Brian went upstairs to his room. He tidied his bed and found the tape he had been looking for in the morning. He put it on and listened to it through his headphones so he wouldn't disturb his Mum. He knew she'd be having a nap after dinner. He hoped Penny would be better tomorrow.

A day in the life of Brian: notes for discussion

Points that might be noted in the daily recording:

- Brian saying to Frank that he wanted to play with the new computer game and then later saying he was bored with computers. There might also be a mention of the response in relation to being asked about Olly.
- Helping to clear up in the garden.
- Playing cards with Martin.

Issues that need to be identified in the Careplan Objectives:

- Supporting Brian in negotiating different relationships within the Resource Centre, e.g. Penny and Olly.
- Purposeful programme of activities so that computer time is ensured.
- Consideration of home circumstances, and how they might be affecting Brian.

Case sheet 2D, Physical disability: A day in the life of Surinder Birdi

Surinder, a Sikh woman of forty eight, waited for the transport. She had heard the clock chime half past nine so she knew it was late. Sometimes it was early, more often it was late. She never really knew when it was going to arrive. Still, the driver was always friendly, well at least his voice seemed pleasant enough. People she had met since the accident, only existed as voices, and smells, and perhaps by their touch, the way they would hold her, confidently or tentatively. She had found the touching alarming at first but now it seemed reassuring.

The doorbell rang. Her daughter went to answer it. Surinder had been grateful for her daughter's help in the last twelve months. It had been a dreadful strain for the girl especially as she was coming up for exams, but she had done well and would be going off to university shortly. Surinder wondered how they would manage after she had gone. Her husband had tried to help, but he was always so busy with his business, and besides, both he and Surinder felt awkward about him assisting with any very personal aspects of her daily care. They had no other children.

Ron, the driver, greeted her and pushed her wheelchair down the path. She waited as the ramp raised her into the back of the transport vehicle. She heard voices around her. They seemed so loud. As she adjusted to the sound she heard her friend Maya calling her name. She had been going to the day centre for six months now and Maya had become a special friend. Maya's voice seemed nervous. She chatted on about her son coming to visit her at the weekend. Surinder wondered if she was imagining Maya's discomfort. All she had was the voice, nothing else to indicate how Maya was feeling.

When Surinder arrived at the day centre, Maya headed off for her cookery session, while Surinder joined the group for sewing and embroidery. She had always enjoyed embroidery and even though she could no longer see the product of her labours, she could feel the stitches and conjure up an image in her head. It gave her some satisfaction. The staff at the centre had tried to get her to learn Braille and then suggested computer skills, but she had found it all too frustrating and had given up. She knew they were disappointed with her and expected her to try harder but what was the point.

It was the same with the wheelchair. She didn't want to go out in it. She was embarrassed. It didn't matter what the staff said, or her husband or her daughter, she would never come to terms with it. She was fed up with all this putting a brave face on it. Some days she just felt like screaming, 'Why me?' Why did she have to be walking down that road at that time or why did that car have to be driving down that road at the same time. She didn't remember anything but she would be living with the consequences for the rest of her life. Did any of them know how desperate she felt sometimes? Her feelings were often in such turmoil, frustrated, angry, desolate, and yet guilty for being so negative and full of self-pity. The staff had tried to talk to her about counselling, but she couldn't share those terrible feelings with anyone else. She felt that if she actually gave voice to them, that would somehow make them more real, and that would make them even more destructive and dangerous.

Surinder quietly sewed for most of the morning. Estelle Monbiot, the instructor, asked her if she was interested in learning patchwork as there were lots of different materials she could work with, which she might find interesting and enjoyable. Surinder felt an instant disinclination to do anything which would just make her more painfully aware of her limitations, and of how difficult it was to learn anything now. She said she would think about it.

Surinder had the lunch she had brought from home warmed up for her. That had been a condition of attending the centre, that she could bring her own food. The staff at the centre had said they could meet her dietary needs but she insisted she preferred home cooking, and she was glad she had, given what she smelled being served up. Her daughter had done all of the cooking after the accident, but gradually Surinder was beginning to become more confident in her own kitchen once more.

Maya sat with Surinder after lunch and told her again about her son coming to visit her. She went on to explain that her son wanted her to move closer to him so he would be able to keep an eye on her. Maya had agreed and he was coming to discuss arrangements. Maya said she would probably be moving in a month. Surinder felt suddenly betrayed. She liked Maya. Maya had become her friend. She could talk to her, something Surinder found difficult with most people and now Maya was going, Surinder didn't know whether to feel angry or sad. She remained quiet and said she would miss Maya. She heard the awkwardness in Maya's voice, saying how she would keep in touch.

Surinder told staff that she had a slight headache and didn't feel up to joining the creative writing group. She had started going three weeks ago. Surinder had few problems with the language after living in England for nearly twenty years, but she didn't really understand the point of the stories and the poetry was a complete mystery. She heard these voices droning on and found the words disappearing into a meaningless noise. Her concentration would falter as she became lost in her own thoughts again.

Surinder wanted to be alone. She asked to be wheeled out to the patio at the back of the day centre. It was quiet there. There was a cool breeze, they wrapped her up and she felt cocooned, strangely removed from everything and everyone around her. This induced a brief sense of calm but suddenly her sense of isolation felt like a physical pain, great torrents of grief overwhelmed her. She felt her whole body convulsing with the emotion. She felt abandoned, helpless before her demons, all the wretched despair welled up inside her. She tried to pray but her prayers were empty gestures in which she no longer found any comfort. She cried and moaned but no one saw or heard her. Everyone was busy with other things.

After half an hour, Tom came out to see how she was. Surinder had regained her composure. She said her headache was worse, but she was alright. Tom chatted about the creative writing group and asked her how it was going. Surinder said she didn't really like it. Tom asked her what she might like to do instead. Surinder said she didn't know.

A day in the life of Surinder Birdi: notes for discussion

Points that might be noted in the daily recording:

- Surinder spent the morning doing embroidery. The option of learning patchwork was suggested by Estelle Monbiot, the instructor. Surinder said she would think about it but did not seem very enthusiastic.
- Surinder complained of a head ache after lunch, and said she did not want to join the creative writing group, which she later said she didn't like.
- Surinder spent time alone on patio.

Issues that need to be identified in the Careplan Objectives:

- Working with feelings about her disabilities in a less formal context than counselling. Surinder is uncomfortable with the idea of counselling and may respond more positively to what she may perceive as a less pressurised approach. Surinder may be more willing to talk about her feelings when she feels a relationship has already been established. Staff, especially her keyworker, may find that more is achieved by themselves building a more trusting relationship with Surinder, than by focusing on the value of counselling.
- There is a danger that in continuing to offer Surinder different options for activities in an attempt to develop her skills and confidence, the approach is having the reverse effect, making Surinder more aware of what she can't do and what she finds difficult and frustrating. The record then reads as a catalogue of failed initiatives and a testimony to Surinder's seemingly negative attitude.
- Perhaps the emphasis needs to be placed on what Surinder can do. She is clearly making progress at home with cooking and maybe that could be developed further. This could then be linked to a strategy for how she will manage when her daughter goes to university.

Training module: The daily log

↗ Objective

The aim of this module is to demonstrate the importance of the daily record, not only as evidence of what has happened and the action taken, but also as a means of effective communication between members of the care team in the delivery of quality care. Learners are asked to examine a series of entries in case material, made over a given period of time in respect of an individual service user, to identify the problems with the different entries and then consider how inadequate or inappropriate recording compromises the quality of care provided. Again, there are different versions and different case sheets for those working with different client groups.

🕐 Timing

Allow 40 minutes for this module.

✏️ Materials

You will need:

- case sheets *The Daily Log*:
  - 3A: Older people in residential care. Ted Hinks
  - 3B: Older people receiving home care. Mr Kolinski
  - 3C: Children and young people in residential care. Sam Babylon
  - 3D: Learning and physical disability in residential care. Karen Horrocks
- paper
- pens
- flipchart and markers

ⓘ Trainer's guidelines

Step 1: allow 5 minutes

Introduce the exercise by explaining it briefly, and divide the participants into groups of two, three or four people. Distribute the appropriate case sheet and ask each group to read through the entries and identify, through group discussion, the problems with each entry. Make it clear that, although the handwriting and lack of proper date and signature may be a problem with some entries, there are additional problems.

Step 2: allow 15 minutes

The participants should work in their small groups on the case sheets.

Step 3: allow 15 minutes

In reviewing the feedback from the groups, the trainer should take each entry in the case sheet in turn, and ask one group to identify the problems with that particular entry. Ask the other groups whether they have found any further problems and add any points yourself, if they have not already been covered.

With the next entry, move on to the next group to lead on the feedback, and then again open it up to the rest of the larger group. Continue this way until all the entries have been discussed.

Points for criticism include:

- assumptions
- speculation
- vague and imprecise descriptions
- judgmental language
- discriminatory statements
- slang or colloquial expressions
- no indication of staff response to situation
- inappropriate abbreviations
- inappropriate references to other service users
- irrelevant detail

As you go through the entries ask the group as a whole how they think the service user in the case sheet, might be feeling.

Step 4: allow 5 minutes

Conclude the exercise by underlining the importance of recording as a communication tool which enables the team to provide effective and consistent care.

Case sheet 3A, Older people in residential care: The daily log. Ted Hinks

Day:	Ted seemed a bit out of sorts today.
Night:	Ted had a night-time drink of Horlicks at about 10.00 p.m., washed and got into bed. He had a restless night.
Day:	Ted provoked an argument with Lionel during the morning. He was rude to care staff when they tried to help and refused to come to the dining room for his meals. He ate in his room.
Night:	Ted went to bed early and would not take his medication. He was up half the night trying to pee.
Day:	Ted has been complaining of feeling unwell and has stayed in bed all day. He's probably still feeling angry about yesterday.
Night:	Ted was very difficult and unreasonable during the night. He kept on pressing the buzzer to complain about Mrs Hodges, who has been very poorly and whose coughing, he said, was keeping him awake.
Day:	Ted was complaining of pain in his abdomen and demanded to see the doctor. Dr Ellis called this morning and couldn't find much wrong with him. Dr Ellis thinks it might possibly be a U.T.I. Please collect a MSU.
Night:	Ted imagines there is something seriously wrong with him. I told him he really would make himself ill if he went on like this.
Day:	Ted's attention seeking behaviour is becoming more of a problem. He is increasingly uncooperative and aggressive. He insists he is in pain and too ill to get up, although he is still eating very well and does not seem very poorly.
Night:	Ted has been lying awake for hours. He fell out of bed at 5.00 a.m.
Day:	Ted was seen by the doctor. He couldn't find anything wrong with him.
Night:	I went into Ted during the night and found he was plastered. It took me ages to clear him up.

Case sheet 3B, Older people receiving home care: The daily log. Mr Kolinski

a.m.:	Assisted Mr Kolinski to wash and dress. Made him breakfast.
p.m.:	Mr Kolinski seemed tired and was ready to go to bed at 10.00 p.m.
a.m.:	Mr Kolinski usual self.
p.m.:	Mr Kolinski said he hadn't eaten his lunch but he does get forgetful.
a.m.:	Mr Kolinski had had a bad night. I left him some breakfast.
p.m.:	Mr Kolinski said he was constipated. I told him not to worry.
a.m.:	Mr Kolinski refused to get up or eat anything and became very abusive when I suggested phoning his daughter. He wanted me to call the doctor.
p.m.:	Mr Kolinski was very bad-tempered. He started going on in Polish so I wouldn't understand him. His daughter had got the prescription but he made out the medicine made him feel sick, although he's had it before without complaining.
a.m.:	Mr Kolinski is still being very difficult, pretending he doesn't understand me, and is making things worse by not taking his medicine. I left him some breakfast but I don't think he's going to eat it.
p.m.:	Mr Kolinski said he hasn't eaten anything again but I think he'd be a lot worse by now if he hadn't.
a.m.:	Mr Kolinski seemed confused and would not speak to me, although he did eat something and took his medicine without any more fuss.
p.m.:	I found Mr Kolinski on the floor in the bathroom and called the ambulance.

Case sheet 3C, Children and young people in residential care: The daily log. Sam Babylon

Friday

evening — Sam came home from school in a foul mood. She refused to eat any dinner and spent the evening in her room.

night — Sam was complaining she couldn't sleep.

Saturday

morning — Sam had an argument with Laura after breakfast. Laura ended up crying. She watched T.V. and then went out.

evening — Sam hasn't returned.

night — Sam came back at 2 a.m. and was very mouthy. She said she'd missed the bus home.

Sunday

morning — Sam laid in bed all morning and got up at lunch time. She said she had a headache and was given some pain-killers.

evening — Sam still complaining of a headache and feeling unwell. She went to bed early.

night — Sam very restless.

Monday

morning — Sam refused to go to school, saying she didn't feel well, although she still wanted breakfast.

evening — Sam very hostile all evening.

night — Sam had a nightmare.

Tuesday

morning — Sam still refusing to go to school, complaining of stomach pains. Appointment made with doctor for Wed.

evening — Sam spent a long time on the phone and was very abusive when Jane wanted to use it and insisted on staying by the phone until it was free. John warned Sam that the phone was for everyone's use.

night — Sam had a drink of hot chocolate at 10.00 p.m., had a warm shower and got ready for bed at 11.30 p.m. She was still awake at 2 a.m. She seems to be worried about something.

Case sheet 3D, Learning and physical disability in residential care: The daily log. Karen Horrocks

Day:	Karen has been playing up all day, shouting and screaming for no reason. The other residents were really fed up.
Night:	Karen had a fitful night.
Day:	Karen was very subdued, probably tired after yesterday. Her mother called and started to complain again about Karen putting on weight. She is always so negative, saying how much better the care home was in Scotland before they moved down south.
Night:	Karen eventually settled after keeping everyone awake half the night.
Day:	Karen ate a good breakfast and was taken for a walk to the park. The wheels on her wheelchair seem to be catching on something and making it difficult to push. Karen enjoyed her lunch. She became excitable when Dominic and Les started messing around and she made herself sick. It went all over the place.
Night:	Karen puked up again in the night.
Day:	Dr Griffiths was called and thinks Karen has a stomach bug. He said to keep her off food and only give her liquids for twenty-four hours. If she's sick again after that, he wants to see her again. Karen has been very challenging with staff all day.
Night:	Karen was very unwilling to go to bed. She deliberately made it awkward for staff to move her and Theresa pulled her back.
Day:	Karen had some lunch and seemed OK. She started screaming again when Dominic and Les came back from their trip into town. She wants to be the centre of attention all the time and hates it when anyone else is around.
Night:	Karen slept for once.
Day:	Karen was difficult all morning. She was taken to the toilet after lunch, became very aggressive with staff and fell on the floor.

Section 6: Writing the Record

Training module: Making a record from transcripts

⬈ Objective

The aim of this module is to explore the problematic nature of interpreting what someone means, from what they say, and how to identify the relevant issues in the recording. The exercise provides learners with a transcript of a discussion between a careworker and a service user, from which they are asked to make an appropriate record. The exercise is designed to stimulate discussion of the difficult questions of judgement which have to be made when identifying the important issues to record, and how the observer's own subjective perception may influence their interpretation of what someone else is saying. Again, the material used is case sheets, and there are different versions for those working with different client groups. For this exercise, the case sheets have two parts: the transcript, the suggested record.

🕐 Timing

Allow 40 minutes for this module.

✎ Materials

You will need:

- case sheets, *Transcripts*:
  - 4A: Older people in residential care. Ashvale Park
  - 4B: Children and young people in residential care. Minsterly Avenue
  - 4C: Learning disability. Jane Gillespie
  - 4D: Mental health. Leo Patterson
  - 4E: Physical disability. Gerry London
  - 4F: Children with physical and learning difficulties. Mrs Chen
- flipchart and markers
- paper
- pens

ⓘ Trainer's guidelines

Step 1: allow 25 minutes

Explain the exercise by way of introduction and give out the appropriate case sheet. Divide participants into groups of between two and four individuals, although this exercise could also be done individually. Ask the participants to make their record from the transcript.

Step 2: allow 20 minutes

Ask the groups to read out their records, and while they are doing that, the trainer needs to note the main points of each record on the flipchart, and then compare with the whole group their different recordings. What was similar, and what was different, and why? Compare the group versions with the suggested record of whichever case sheet has been used. Clarify why certain points needed to be included in the record. Participants sometimes get side tracked into evaluating the effectiveness of the worker's intervention, but the object of the exercise is not to pass an opinion on the worker or to go beyond an account of the actual transcript. It may well be that participants will make certain judgements and interpretations of what they think certain statements might actually signify but that goes beyond the remit of the exercise. That constitutes a second stage where the worker goes on to give their professional opinion, which would obviously be based on a much deeper and more comprehensive knowledge of the individual service user.

Case sheet 4A, Older people in residential care: Transcript. Ashvale Park

Resident: Mrs Emily Davies
Keyworker: Dominique Severin

Background

Mrs Davies, a retired teacher, aged 84, has lived at Ashvale for five years. She had to give up her own home after suffering a stroke, which very much reduced her mobility. Failing eyesight has further restricted her independence. Her daughter lives in Scotland and only visits two or three times a year. Mrs Davies is a quiet lady, who has made a number of friends with other residents sharing similar interests to her own. She used to enjoy the theatre and still likes to read, although her poor eyesight is making this more difficult.

Dominique is helping Mrs Davies to get dressed in the morning.

Dialogue

Mrs Davies: *Oh, I don't know dear, I feel so very tired this morning. I didn't sleep very well last night. I kept waking up. I never used to have problems at night but I suppose it's just another thing you have to learn to get on with.*

Dominique: *You do seem to be having more problems with sleeping recently. Do you think it might help to see the doctor? He might be able to give you something.*

Mrs Davies: *I don't want anything like that. I've never taken tablets, not like some people. I think they just cause other problems. Look at Alice. I don't know how many different things she takes and none of it seems to do her much good. No, my dear, I don't think tablets are the answer.*

Dominique: *Well, do you think there is anything else that might help?*

Mrs Davies: *It's no use, I'm just getting old. I always used to read before I went off to sleep but I can't really see the print that well now. It's getting more and more difficult even in the daylight. You know I always used to say, that's the one thing I wouldn't be without, my eyes.*

Dominique: *What about the talking books we can get from the library?*

Mrs Davies: *I know they're a very good idea, but you know the selection is very limited. I did try but there was nothing very much that I found interesting, lots of popular fiction but I always really liked biographies.*

Dominique: *Well, let me have another word with the library and see if they can suggest something.*

Mrs Davies: *That's very kind of you dear. I know you mean well, but it's very hard, you know, when you get to my age, relying on other people all the time. I always did things for myself. I was very independent when I was younger, but in the end it makes little difference. It's our bodies that let us down. They say it's all a question of attitude but it's not easy when everything's just wearing out. The trouble is, we were never meant to grow this old. We're no use to anyone anymore. We're not much use to ourselves.*

Dominique: *Oh, this doesn't sound like you Emily. What about your daughter, and your grandchildren, and your friends?*

Mrs Davies: *I know dear, I expect I'm just feeling a bit sorry for myself but I know Lisa can't be running down from Scotland any more than she does. She and the children have their own lives to lead without me being a burden. And as for Alice and Elsie, well they're even worse than me. Look at Elsie, she wears herself out just walking a few yards. We're all on our last legs. It's not much fun getting old.*

Dominique: *You usually sound so positive.*

Mrs Davies: *Well I try, because I suppose that's all you can do really but it's not easy. I miss the things I used to be able to do, the things I took for granted then. I don't want to be the way I am now. And you don't like to look too far into the future.*

Dominique: *What do you mean?*

Mrs Davies: *Well, nothing is going to get any better and I do get frightened thinking what might happen. I don't want to end up helpless. That's my real dread. Not being able to do anything for myself. I don't want that, but you can't do anything about it, can you? They put animals out of their misery, but not people.*

Dominique: *Well not in this country anyway, and there is a lot that can be done to make things easier for someone if they do reach that stage. And I'm not sure that you could be really certain what someone wanted. People do change their minds.*

Mrs Davies: *Yes, I know it's very difficult and I probably am just feeling out of sorts. It doesn't help lying awake at night. All sorts of things come into your head. Anyway, my dear, you've spent far too long listening to all my moans.*

Dominique: *I will have to go and help Alice, but maybe we can talk about this again.*

Mrs Davies: *Oh, don't mind me dear, there's others here with far worse problems than me.*

Case sheet 4A, Older people in residential care: Suggested record. Ashvale Park

Resident: Mrs Emily Davies
Keyworker: Dominique Severin

Mrs Davies said she has been having problems sleeping. I suggested she see the doctor but she does not want any medication.

Mrs Davies used to read before she slept but her eyesight is now making it difficult to read even through the day. I suggested talking books but she feels the selection is limited. I suggested I would explore further.

Mrs Davies also expressed concerns about her increasing dependence and fear of the future, of not being able to do anything for herself. 'They put animals out of their misery, but not people'.

I offered reassurance, and said I would talk with her about this again.

Case sheet 4B, Children and young people in residential care: Transcript. Minsterly Avenue

Young Person: Dawn Samtani
Worker: Rita Fawzi

Background

Dawn is a fourteen-year-old girl who has been in residential care for 12 months after her mother moved to Spain with a new boyfriend, abandoning Rita and her brother, George, aged ten. George has been placed in foster care but Dawn was initially resistant, saying she had had enough of families and refused to consider a foster placement. Recently she has become increasingly frustrated in her residential home, finding it difficult to get on with some of the other young people in the home. She is now willing to look at a foster placement and has met a family with two teenage children, Phil aged 18 and Viki aged 16.

Rita is in the office, drawing up the staff rotas for next month. Dawn asks to speak with her.

Dialogue

Dawn:	*Have you got a minute?*
Rita:	*Well, I'm doing the rotas at the moment. What do you want?*
Dawn:	*I'm seeing Terry (Dawn's social worker) tomorrow and I'm not sure what to say to him.*
Rita:	*What do you mean?*
Dawn:	*You know about the Frazers. He'll want to know what I thought, if I liked them.*
Rita:	*Well, what did you think about them?*
Dawn:	*I don't know really. I mean they were alright, they tried to be really nice but I don't know.*
Rita:	*You went with Kieran didn't you? Have you talked with him about it?*
Dawn:	*Yeah, well, sort of, Kieran's alright but you know I can't really talk to him. He thought they were really nice. I wanted you to go with me but you were off sick and Terry couldn't come because there was some emergency somewhere, so Kieran was the only one who could go.*
Rita:	*But Kieran is your keyworker now.*

Dawn: *Yeah, but I didn't really want him. I liked Yvonne (previous keyworker who left for another job), and after she went, I got stuck with Kieran 'cause he didn't have enough people.*

Rita: *Well, OK, I know it's not always easy in these situations but Kieran is a lot more understanding than you think.*

Dawn: *I don't care. I didn't want him as my keyworker and I don't want to talk to him about going to the Frazers. I want to talk to you, right, but if you're (shouting) not fucking interested then you can fuck off. (Moving towards the door.) You're all the same you lot, just a lot of tossers, it's just a job to you.*

Rita: *Alright Dawn, calm down. I'm sorry if I seemed as though I didn't want to talk, it's just I thought it would be better if you spoke with Kieran, but it's obviously important you talk about this. Sit down and tell me what happened with the Frazers.*

Dawn: *Are you sure you can spare the fucking time?*

Rita: *Do you want some tea?*

Dawn: *No, it's all right. (Sitting down) I don't know what I really want. Part of me wants to stay here, but then I think of some of the wankers living here and I know I've got to get out. But then when I went to see the Frazers I felt like I didn't belong. Like I said, they were trying to be nice and all that but it didn't seem real.*

Rita: *It's obviously a very strange situation where everyone is going to find it difficult to just relax and be themselves. These things take time. Terry won't be expecting you to have made a decision by tomorrow. He'll be more interested in whether you want to get to know them any better or whether you really didn't like them and there's no point in seeing them again.*

Dawn: *I quite liked them, although I'm not sure about their daughter. She looked a bit of a stuck up cow to me but Phil seemed a good laugh. I liked him. It's difficult 'cause I think if I agree to see them again I'm sort of saying I'm interested and then it's going to be harder if in the end I don't want to go.*

Rita: *It's hard to give something or someone a chance because it might not turn out as you wanted and then you might be disappointed.*

Dawn: *Sort of, but it's difficult 'cause you don't really know what you want and what you really feel.*

Rita: *Dawn, I think it's very natural for you to feel like that. This could be a very big step for you and it's understandable that you're unsure, and afraid that it might not work out. But you can take things slowly. Nobody is going to force you to make a decision before you're ready. It's good that your first impression of the*

> Frazers was positive but you need time to get to know them better and for them to get to know you.

Dawn: *Yeah, I guess so. They had a really nice house. I liked that, although they had two dogs and I've never really liked dogs. These were small though. I suppose I could get used to them. They had funny tea, smelled weird. She was nice though, Mrs Frazer, she seemed kind. Her husband works in a bank. I think he's a manager or something.*

Telephone rings.

Rita: *(answering telephone) Oh hi Tim . . . pause . . . you do sound bad. No, it's probably best you stay at home in the warm. This bug seems to be doing the rounds. Thanks for letting me know. Hope you're feeling better soon.*

Dawn: *Is that Tim? Isn't he working tonight then. He was supposed to be bringing in a magazine for me.*

Rita: *No, he's not well and I'm going to have to try and get someone to cover. How are you feeling now, Dawn?*

Dawn: *Better.*

Rita: *Do you think we need to talk anymore before you see Terry tomorrow?*

Dawn: *No, it's OK, I'll see Terry tomorrow and ask him to sort out another visit.*

Case sheet 4B, Children and young people in residential care: Suggested record. Minsterly Avenue

Young Person: Dawn Samtani
Worker: Rita Fawzi

Dawn wanted to discuss her visit to the Frazers (prospective foster family) as she will be seeing Terry Young (her social worker) tomorrow.

I suggested that it might be more appropriate for her to talk to her keyworker Kieran, especially as he accompanied her on the visit; but she says she can't really talk to him and became angry, saying 'It's just a job to you' when she felt I wasn't interested. (Dawn's expressed feelings need to be noted even though there may be various interpretations placed on their significance and meaning. Does she really not get on with Kieran or is she instead looking for reassurance and some indication that people care about her?)

Dawn was unsure about her feelings in relation to the Frazers. She quite liked them, especially Mrs Frazer and Phil, the son, but she did not seem to like the daughter. She liked the house and felt she could get used to the dogs, even though she had never really liked dogs. She was worried that if she said she wanted to see the family again, she would be committing herself and she wasn't sure what she really wanted.

I reassured her that it was natural to feel uncertain about such an important step and understandable that she was worried that it might not work out, which is why Terry would not be expecting her to rush into making a decision too quickly.

The discussion was cut short by a member of staff ringing in sick. I asked Dawn if she needed to talk anymore and she said 'No' and that she would ask Terry to arrange a further visit to the Frazers.

Case sheet 4C, Learning disability: Transcript. Home visit to Jane Gillespie

Background

Jane is a 29-year-old woman with learning disability. She lives with her mother. They have recently moved to be nearer to Jane's married sister. Jane's father died when she was thirteen. Jane was upset to have to leave the resource centre she used to attend, and required some persuasion by her mother to consider going to a similar centre near to her new home.

You visited Jane to arrange her place at the resource centre and were confident that she would make a successful adjustment. Last Friday you had a message from one of the workers at the resource centre that there had been an incident involving Jane, where she had become very upset and her mother had to be called at work to come and fetch her and take her home. You have also received a message that Jane's mother has called and wants to see you urgently.

You speak to the manager of the resource centre, who tells you that Jane had arrived for her first day at the resource centre on Monday 17th September, appearing a little nervous and rather quiet but she began to relax as people started to talk to her. Just before lunchtime Jane had become very upset following an incident with Robert, another member from a local residential home, attending the centre. It was not entirely clear what had happened but Jane had claimed that Robert had tried to follow her into the toilet and had said rude things to her and then tried to grab her, although she was too upset to give a very clear account of what had actually taken place. Robert had become very angry when he was asked what had happened and said Jane was just telling lies because she didn't like him. Jane wanted to leave the centre immediately but was persuaded to wait for her mother to collect her. Subsequent discussion with Robert had not yielded any further information.

You arrange to visit Jane and her mother at home on Monday 24th September. It is clear from talking to Mrs Gillespie on the phone that she is very unhappy about what happened to her daughter and feels the centre is to blame. She said she is considering making a formal complaint.

Dialogue

Simon: *Good morning, Mrs Gillespie*

Mrs Gillespie: *Good morning, Simon. Thank you for coming. Jane's upstairs at the moment. She still feels very embarrassed about talking about what happened, so she wanted me to see you first.*

Simon:	*I'm really sorry that Jane is feeling so upset about all this. I don't want to make things more difficult but it would help to know what happened exactly. The account she gave to the staff at the centre was not very clear.*
Mrs Gillespie:	*Well, when I arrived to pick her up she was still in tears and didn't really want to say anything, except that she didn't want to ever go back again and that Robert had been horrible. She just wanted to go home, and when we got back she went up to her room and played her music for the rest of the afternoon. She wouldn't say anything to me.*
Simon:	*Has she said anything about the incident since then?*
Mrs Gillespie:	*Well, yes, but it comes out in bits and pieces. It seems she had been working in the greenhouse. She's always enjoyed working with plants and growing things, just like her Dad. She had been helping to pot up seedlings with another girl called Marion. They had been getting on very well. I gather Marion was a lot older and had been going to the centre for a number of years. She was telling Jane about the different things that went on. Robert was also working in the greenhouse. He seemed very friendly at first and Jane quite liked him. She said she thought he was funny and she had been laughing at his jokes, but she didn't know what to do when he followed her into the toilet. She told him to go out but he wouldn't and said how pretty she was and how he wanted to kiss her. She usually starts to become anxious again at this point in the story and only says that he tried to grab her and that she pushed him away. She's not very confident with boys, never has been. She's quite innocent, just like a little girl really.*
Simon:	*How has she been in herself during the past week?*
Mrs Gillespie:	*Well, she's been very moody, not her usual self at all. But then it has been awkward, I've had to have time off work with it all and my other daughter has had Jane over her place to keep an eye on her. It's not ideal because Kathleen has a young baby and has her hands full anyway. Jane's always glad to come home but what else can I do? She's definite she doesn't want to go back to the centre. I mean I'm not very happy about the idea myself and I do think they have a lot to answer for but at the same time it's going to very difficult if she won't go back.*
Simon:	*Yes, I can see that. Do you think Jane might be willing to come down and talk to me now?*
Mrs Gillespie:	*Well I can see, but I don't know.*

Mrs Gillespie returns with Jane

Mrs Gillespie: *This is Simon, Jane. Do you remember you spoke to him when we first moved here?*

Jane: *Hello.*

Simon: *Hello Jane. Thank you for coming down. I hope I'm not interrupting anything.*

Jane: *No, it's alright. I just had my tapes on.*

Simon: *What were you listening to?*

Jane: *All Saints, I really like them.*

Simon: *They're a bit like the Spice Girls aren't they?*

Jane: *Yeah, but they're better. The Spice Girls are boring now.*

Simon: *Anyway, Jane, I wanted to speak to you about the centre, and what happened with Robert, if that's alright. It's important that we know what happened although I can understand that you might find it difficult to talk about.*

Jane: *I don't like Robert. I don't want to see him ever again.*

Simon: *But what did you think of the centre before the incident with Robert? Did you like the other people there?*

Jane: *Yeah I liked it. The other people were nice.*

Simon: *Your Mum told me that you liked Robert first of all, when you were working together in the greenhouse.*

Jane: *He was nice then. He told funny jokes. He made me laugh.*

Simon: *How long were you working in the greenhouse with Robert?*

Jane: *I don't know. We went in there after coffee, Marion and me. Robert came in after.*

Simon: *What happened when you left the greenhouse?*

Jane: *I wanted a pee. Robert followed me to the toilets. I told him to go away but he came in after me.*

Simon: *What happened then?*

Jane: (looking at the floor, clenching and unclenching her hands) *He started saying stupid things? I told him to shut up, but he wouldn't. I said I'd tell the staff and he said he didn't care. I said I didn't like him anymore but he carried on being stupid, so I pushed him and ran out.*

Simon: *Did anything else happen?*

Jane:	(continuing looking at the floor) *I don't want to talk about it. I don't want to see him again. He's a pig.*
Simon:	*What do you mean, he's a pig?*
Jane:	*I don't like him.*
Simon:	*I know it might be difficult to talk about some things but it is important for us to know exactly what Robert did.*
Jane:	(starting to shout) *I've told you what happened. I don't want to talk about it anymore. Alright?* (Jane gets up and leaves the room).
Simon:	*I'm sorry, I didn't mean to upset her but I did feel it was important to press her on the details.*
Mrs Gillespie:	*Well, that's all I've got out of her. I would like her to go back to the centre but I don't know how to persuade her to go back. She just gets so angry when I even suggest it. Clearly this Robert character really upset her. I mean, I don't know what the staff were doing to allow them to carry on unsupervised like that. Where were they, that's what I'd like to know?*
Simon:	*I can understand that you're very concerned. It's very difficult though, if Jane is so against going back.*
Mrs Gillespie:	*Well, I think more happened in those toilets than Jane's saying and I don't think that Robert should be allowed there. I'm sure Jane would go back if she knew he wasn't there.*
Simon:	*It's difficult to take the matter any further at the moment, if Jane will not say anymore. I'll have another word with staff at the centre and get back to you by the end of the week.*
Mrs Gillespie:	*OK then, well, thanks again for coming. I hope you can sort this out for us. Bye then.*
Simon:	*Bye.*

Case sheet 4C, Learning disability: Suggested record. Home visit to Jane Gillespie

Home Visit to Jane Gillespie
Worker: Simon Williams
24th September 2000

On arrival I was told by Mrs Gillespie that Jane was upstairs, and that Jane wanted her mother to talk to me first as Jane felt very embarrassed talking about the incident in the day centre. I explained that it was important that I found out exactly what had happened.

Mrs Gillespie then provided the following account:

Jane was in tears when she picked her up from the centre, saying that she never wanted to go back again and that Robert had been horrible. When they arrived back home Jane went to her room and would not say anything more.

Jane has gradually said a little more since then. Jane had been working in the greenhouse with Marion and Robert. Jane liked Robert and had been laughing at his jokes but she didn't know what to do when he followed her into the toilet. She told him to go out but he wouldn't and said how pretty she was and how he wanted to kiss her. Mrs Gillespie says that Jane usually becomes anxious at this point and says that Robert tried to grab her and she pushed him away

Mrs Gillespie said that Jane had been moody since the incident. There are problems in that Kathleen, Jane's sister, who has recently had a baby, has been looking after Jane while Mrs Gillespie is at work and it would therefore be difficult if Jane could not go back to the centre.

Mrs Gillespie then asked Jane to join us.

I explained to Jane that I needed her to tell me what had happened at the centre. Jane said she didn't like Robert and didn't want to see him again. Asked about what she thought about the centre before the incident, she said she liked it and she thought the 'people were nice.'

She said that Robert had been nice in the greenhouse, had told funny jokes and made her laugh. He followed her to the toilets. She told him to go away but he came in after her. Asked what happened next, Jane looked at the floor, clenching and unclenching her hands. She said that Robert had started to 'say stupid things'. She said, 'I told him to shut up but he wouldn't.' She said, 'I'd tell the staff but he said he didn't care.' She said, 'I didn't like him anymore but he carried on being stupid and so I pushed him and ran out.'

When asked if anything else happened, Jane said, 'I don't want to talk about it. I don't want to see him again. He's a pig.' Asked what she meant by 'he's a pig', Jane said 'I don't like him' and said she had told me what had happened and she didn't want to talk about it anymore. At that point Jane left the room.

Mrs Gillespie says that Jane has become angry when she has suggested Jane return to the centre. Mrs Gillespie feels that more happened in the toilets than Jane is saying. She questioned why they were left unsupervised by the staff, and feels that Robert should not be allowed back to the centre.

I said I would speak again to staff at the centre and get back to her by Friday 28 September.

(N.B. This level of detail is necessary when there is such a potentially serious matter at issue. It is not clear what took place in the toilets. It may be that Jane is making it up, or possibly she was sexually assaulted. The implications are serious. Mrs Gillespie may be making a formal complaint. It is therefore crucial to record everything that is said in relation to describing the incident.)

Case sheet 4D, Mental health: Transcript. Home visit to Leo Patterson

Background

Leo is 23 and was diagnosed with Schizophrenia twelve months ago.

Worker: Christine Weeks
Thursday 4th January 2000

Dialogue

Christine: *Good morning, Mrs Patterson.*

Mrs P: *Good morning, Christine.*

Christine: *How are you today?*

Mrs P: *Not so good, I'm very worried about Leo. He's stopped taking his medication.*

Christine: *Is he here this morning? I've heard that he hasn't been attending the day centre for the last few weeks. I was wondering what was going on.*

Mrs P: *No, he's gone out, and I don't know where. He's become very secretive again. He won't tell me what he's been up to. Just stays in his room for hours and then goes out without saying anything. I'm sure he's started cutting himself again. He won't let me see his arms but I've noticed blood on his clothes.*

Christine: *How long ago did you notice that?*

Mrs P: *I'm not sure really, I think it's probably about four weeks. I think it was after he had a big row with his Dad.*

Christine: *Have Leo and his Dad been having problems again?*

Mrs P: *Well, you know what Sid's like. He hasn't got any patience and he doesn't really understand. He reckons that as soon as Leo starts managing a bit better, he should be trying to get a job. I tried to tell him it's not fair on Leo, that he's not well. He thinks because Leo seems a bit better the problem has been sorted. But I remember what my cousin was like. It was the same thing, and he never really got any better. Sid reckons it was all my Aunty's fault. He thinks she just spoilt my cousin, let him get away with everything and so he never learnt to stand on his own feet. I try and tell him that it's not as simple as that but he doesn't want to listen. I tell you between the two of them I'll be the next one to be carted off.*

Christine: *It sounds as though you are finding it very difficult managing with Leo at the moment.*

Mrs P: *Well, like I told you, he's come off the medication and he's stopped going to the day centre, and it seems like there's no one really responsible for him, except me, and I don't know what to do. I mean, I can't make him do anything if he doesn't want to. But the thought of him getting really bad again, like he was before. I don't think I can face all that again. I can't understand why you lot can't at least make him stick to his medication.*

Christine: *Well, Leo did seem to be making good progress. The staff at the day centre were very pleased with how he had settled in. He was even making friends with some of the other clients, but then he suddenly stopped attending.*

Mrs P: *I was really disappointed. I did try and persuade him but it was no good and then I realised he was off the medication and he's just going downhill now and I just feel helpless.*

(At this moment Leo comes in through the front door.)

Mrs P: *Leo, is that you?*

Leo: *Yeah.*

Mrs P: *Leo, Christine Weeks, you know the lady who comes to see how you are getting on, is here. She wants to talk to you.*

Leo: *I don't want to talk to anyone.*

(Leo starts to go upstairs. Mrs P goes out to the hall, followed by Christine. Leo is clutching a large plastic bag. He avoids looking at either his mother or Christine and continues to stare at his feet.)

Christine: *Hello, Leo. I just wanted to know how you were at the moment, only I haven't seen you for a while.*

Mrs P: *Oh, come on Leo, at least come and talk to Christine, you know she's here to try and help you.*

Leo: *I don't want anyone's fucking help. They all just make me feel worse. Just leave me alone will you.*

Mrs P: *Leo, it's no good going on like this. You know you'll just end up bad again.*

Christine: *It's all right, Mrs Patterson. I can understand that Leo might not want to talk to me. Would it help if we just sat down and had a cup of coffee together?*

Mrs P: *That's a good idea, I'll go and put the kettle on.*

Leo: (shouting) *I don't want any fucking coffee, didn't you hear. Why do you keep going on? I just want to be quiet. All you do is talk about me. Just go away, all of you.*

(Leo runs up the rest of the stairs and disappears into his room, slamming the door behind him.)

Mrs P: *Well, I'm sorry about that. I'm really sorry. He just seems to be like that a lot of the time now. I can't get any sense out of him.*

Christine: *I realise it's upsetting but I'm glad I've seen him. Clearly things are deteriorating, and so I need to report this back to the team. Is there anything else you want to talk about?*

Mrs P: *Well no, not really, except I suppose I am a bit worried, I mean he never really got nasty before but this time he seems to have such a temper on him.*

Christine: *How bad a temper?*

Mrs P: *Well, he's starting throwing things, you know, like furniture. That's really got Sid mad. He nearly hit Leo the other night.*

Christine: *That sounds quite serious. As I say, I do need to take this back to the team and discuss what we can do next. I know that's not a lot of comfort at the moment but we are trying to help Leo. I'll be in touch by the end of the week.*

Case sheet 4D, Mental health: Suggested record. Home visit to Leo Patterson

Home visit to Leo Patterson

Worker: Christine Weeks
4th January 2000

When I arrived, Leo was not at home. I spoke with Mrs Patterson who is worried about Leo. He is going out and not saying where he has been, although she knows he has not been to the day centre for four weeks.

She says that he has come off his medication, been staying in his room for hours and she thinks he has started cutting himself again. Leo will not let her see his arms, but she has noticed blood on his clothes for the past four weeks.

Mrs Patterson says that Leo had a row with his father four weeks ago, after his father said that he should get a job. Mrs Patterson feels that Leo will go downhill without his medication, and can't understand why Leo can't be made to take it. She is finding the situation more difficult to cope with.

Leo returned home during the visit, clutching a large plastic bag but did not want to talk to me. He stared at his feet while we were talking with him, and when pressed by his mother to have a coffee and talk to me, he became angry, shouting that he 'just wanted to be quiet' and for everyone to go away. He ran upstairs to his room.

Mrs Patterson also said that Leo had developed a temper and had started throwing furniture around, which nearly resulted in his father hitting him.

I said I would take all this information back to the team and that we would be discussing what we could do next to help Leo and that I would be in touch, by the end of next week, 12th January.

Case sheet 4E, Physical disability: Transcript. Home visit to Gerry London

Background

Gerry London is a thirty-five year old man who was involved in a motorbike accident two years ago. He uses a wheelchair, has no movement in his right arm and only has some limited movement in his left arm. He relies on Home Carers for his personal care who visit three times a day. He recently developed pneumonia and was in hospital for four weeks. He was discharged eight weeks ago and this is your second visit to monitor how he is managing.

Client: Gerry London
Worker: David Winter
Date: 24.9.00

Dialogue

David: *Good morning, Gerry, how are you?*

Gerry: *Not so bad really, bit tired.*

David: *Why is that? Have you been sleeping OK?*

Gerry: *Yeah, I suppose so, sometimes it's difficult to get comfortable but yeah I'm sleeping alright. It's just I don't seem to have any energy. I thought I might be feeling a bit better by now.*

David: *Well, you were quite poorly so it's going to take a little while to really get over that.*

Gerry: *I guess I'm just feeling fed up with myself. I've been stuck in the house for ages now. I'm bored but you know I can't be bothered to make the effort to do anything. So I just sit here watching the TV and that just makes me feel worse.*

David: *Well, there's always Riverside Park Day Centre, if you want to get out a bit.*

Gerry: *No thanks, I've been offered that before, but I don't fancy going somewhere like that. I think that would really get me down. I've got enough with my own problems.*

David: *How have you been managing since I last came to see you, that was only a couple of days after you had come out of hospital?*

Gerry: *I'm doing more for myself than I was then, but I still rely on Pat and Brenda a lot more than I did.*

David: *Yes, I thought we might be reviewing what you need now, but I gather that they are still doing as much as when you first came out of hospital.*

Gerry: *I know, I thought I would have made more progress by now but I still feel like an invalid.*

David: *Has the doctor been to see you recently?*

Gerry: *Yeah, he came out last week, because I wasn't feeling very well, and I was worried, but he said I was alright, no temperature or anything and it cleared up in a couple of days. He reckons I've made a good recovery, but I just haven't managed to get back to where I was: and that wasn't that great.*

David: *What do you mean?*

Gerry: *Well, look at me, two years ago I was a real man, I had a good life, a good job. I liked playing football. I could do what I wanted. I had girl friends. Now what have I got?*

David: *I know it's not easy and it takes time adjusting and in some ways two years isn't very long. What sort of support have you got from friends and family?*

Gerry: *Well, Mum has not been well herself recently and Dad and I have never been close. He comes round every couple of months, but never says very much. My brother has this job where he's never home, always off somewhere, earning a fortune, lucky sod. We have a laugh when he's around, go out together, but like I said, he's busy most of the time.*

David: *What about friends?*

Gerry: *Yeah, I've got mates but most of them are married now with kids and they have their own lives to get on with. I think when they do come round now it's because they think they should, because they feel guilty if they don't. I don't think it's because they really want to see me. I mean, I'm not exactly brilliant company, am I?*

David: *You are being very hard on yourself.*

Gerry: *I'm being realistic.*

David: *You may say it's being realistic but perhaps there are still a lot of strong feelings about what has happened which are getting in the way of your being able to move on, to move forward.*

Gerry: *I had all the counselling after the accident but it doesn't change anything does it? I'm still stuck in this wheelchair.*

David: *Talking about how you feel can't change what has happened, but it might help you to look at it differently. You might find it helpful to try counselling again because I think the issues are not the same as when you first had the accident and you were still coping with the shock of what had happened. You are now at the stage where you have experienced the consequences, and perhaps need some help in dealing with them.*

Gerry: *I don't know, maybe you've got a point but I'm not sure. The pneumonia and being in hospital did shake me up a bit and maybe I just need a bit of time to sort myself out again.*

David: *You may be right but perhaps you might like to think about what I've said.*

Gerry: *Yeah, OK, I know you mean well but I'm not sure I want to start churning a lot of stuff over again.*

David: *I can understand that. We can talk about this again if you like. I'll come out and see how things are going in another couple of months. I'll leave the home care arrangements as they are for the time being and we'll see how you go on. If you change your mind about the counselling, or even the day centre, give me a ring.*

Gerry: *OK Thanks. Bye.*

Case sheet 4E, Physical disability:2 Suggested record. Home visit to Gerry London

Home visit to Gerry London

Worker: David Winter
24th September 2000
Purpose of visit: to review progress since last visit 26th July 2000.

Gerry is still feeling tired, lacking energy and is finding it difficult to regain his previous level of functioning. He still relies on Home Care input, as much as he did when he was discharged. He seemed fed up, saying he 'couldn't be bothered to make the effort to do anything'. He has not been out of the house for sometime but was not interested in Riverside Day Centre when I suggested it.

The doctor called last week after Gerry felt unwell, but did not find anything wrong and Gerry said he felt better after a few days.

When asked about family support, he said his mother had been unwell recently and although he saw his father about every two months, they were 'not close'. He had a good relationship with his brother but he worked away a lot of the time.

He felt that friends came round to visit out of a sense of obligation, because they felt 'guilty'.

I suggested that Gerry might find it useful to talk to a counsellor as I felt that there were still some strong feelings he had about the accident which were making it difficult for him to move forward.

He said he had had counselling after the accident but that it did not change his situation. I suggested that maybe there were different issues to discuss now. He wasn't sure but thought I 'might have a point'. Gerry prefers for the moment to see how he gets on in the next few months and said he 'wasn't sure he wanted to start churning a lot of stuff over again'.

I said that I would see him in another couple of months and I would leave the home care support as it is for the time being. I also said that if he changed his mind about the counselling or the day centre to contact me.

Case sheet 4F, Children with physical and learning difficulties: Transcript. Home visit to Mrs Chen

Background

Jin Chen arrived in Britain from Hong Kong with his family ten years ago. He was two years old and his brother was five. Mr Chen set up in business. A sister was born eight years ago. About a year after his sister was born, Jin contracted Meningitis, which resulted in brain damage, leaving Jin severely disabled, unable to walk, with difficulty in co-ordinating his hand and arm movements, limited speech and a degree of mental impairment. Mrs Chen continued to look after Jin at home although she found this a considerable strain while also caring for his younger sister.

Eventually Mrs Chen collapsed with physical exhaustion. She was persuaded by her doctor to look at the option of respite care for Jin, and for the last five years he has been attending Ridgeway House, a local social services respite unit for one week a month, where he has, for most of the time, been very happy. Mrs Chen has been very satisfied with the service until six months ago, following an incident where another child attending the unit had hit Jin, causing bruising to his right arm. Since the incident she thinks that Jin has become more anxious and fearful. Mrs Chen says that she has tried to raise her concerns with staff but she feels they think she is just making a fuss. She has said she will not return Jin to Ridgeway House and she is going to make a formal complaint. You, Shelia White have just taken over the case from a social worker who has recently taken early retirement on health grounds.

Dialogue

Sheila: *Good morning, Mrs Chen.*

Mrs Chen: *Thank you for coming. Please come in. Would you like something to drink? Some tea or coffee?*

Sheila: *No thanks, I've just had one.*

Mrs Chen: *Or perhaps some water?*

Sheila: *No really, it's very kind of you but I'm OK.*

Mrs Chen: *Well, thank you for coming to see me, although I'm not sure how you can help. Mrs Appleby was always very nice but I haven't seen her for a while. I think she's been off sick.*

Sheila: *Yes, she has left the department now, and I have taken over Jin's case. I've been reading Jin's file and I also spoke to the manager at the unit, who is quite concerned about the situation.*

Mrs Chen: *Well, they have never seemed concerned when I have tried to speak to them. This is the problem, I don't feel anyone wants to know. I don't want to be rude but I feel that I have just been ignored.*

Sheila: *Well, it would help if you could tell me, from your point of view, what has been going on.*

Mrs Chen: *Well, as you know it all started six months ago when Jin was punched by that other boy. He had a big bruise on his arm for ages. They phoned me at the time but told me there was nothing to worry about, but I was shocked when I went to collect him two days later. It was a horrible bruise and Jin was upset. He wasn't his usual smiling self, he was very quiet. He didn't want the arm to be touched. The staff told me he had been all right, but I know my son. I was very unhappy about sending him back there, but my husband said that if I tried to manage Jin all on my own again, I wouldn't be able to cope. So he went back for his next visit. He didn't seem pleased to be going. Anyway, nothing happened that I was aware of but I still thought Jin seemed quieter than he normally is.*

Sheila: *Was there anything else which made you think Jin wasn't very pleased to be going back to the unit?*

Mrs Chen: *Well, it's little things, but before when I've talked about the unit, he has responded happily, telling me in his way what he has done and what happened. He doesn't seem to want to talk about it. He just seems much quieter.*

Sheila: *When did you raise your concerns with the staff?*

Mrs Chen: *Well, after another two visits with Jin still not his old self, I asked to speak to the manager. She said it would be better if I spoke to Jin's key worker, but I felt it was something the manager should be concerned with. She said she thought it was probably Jin's age and that he seemed OK when she saw him in the unit. She said he always seemed to have a good appetite.*

Sheila: *So what happened after that?*

Mrs Chen: *Well, I spoke to Jin's key worker but she is only very young and I don't think she really understands Jin.*

Sheila: *What makes you say that?*

Mrs Chen: *Well, she looked as though she had just finished school and I don't think she has really spent that much time with Jin. She didn't know how much he still likes a bed time story.*

Sheila: *What else has made you concerned about Jin's stays at the unit?*

Mrs Chen: *Well, the thing that made me very angry was when I called to pick him up in May and I arrived a bit earlier than usual, and when the member of staff took me through to where Jin was, we found Jin with a group of other children and one of them was poking Jin and shouting at him. Jin looked very frightened. The member of staff just told the other child to stop it. When the child carried on, he was simply given something else to play with, nothing else was done.*

Sheila: *What do you think should have been done?*

Mrs Chen: *The child should have been told off properly and it should have been explained that you don't behave like that.*

Sheila: *Some of the children at Ridgeway House have very limited understanding.*

Mrs Chen: *But they shouldn't be allowed to bully other children. I've had this before with my eldest son, other children bullying him, calling him names because he looks different. It won't stop unless people do something.*

Sheila: *Did you say anything at the time?*

Mrs Chen: *Yes, I complained to the member of staff, and to the manager but they said it was no more than a bit of teasing. I felt very angry.*

Sheila: *I understand that you have not taken Jin back to Ridgeway House since then.*

Mrs Chen: *No, well, we had planned to take Jin with us on holiday in June anyway, and after we came back I talked it over with my husband, and I said I could not take Jin back to that place if he was not going to be looked after any better.*

Sheila: *What does your husband think?*

Mrs Chen: *He is worried about how I will cope but he knows when my mind is made up.*

Sheila: *Do you think it might help if you met with the staff to try and talk about this?*

Mrs Chen: *What is the point? I have tried to talk to them before, but they have always ignored me. They think I am just making a fuss.*

Sheila: *So is there anything more I can do?*

Mrs Chen: *I don't know. I do intend making a complaint about Ridgeway House because I don't think children should have to put up with being bullied but I am worried as well that Jin will become bored at home all the time with me. I don't know that I can* *cope with looking after him all the time, especially as he is getting bigger. The other children have also been happy to have more of my attention when Jin is not here, so it will be difficult for everyone but I can't bring myself to take Jin back there.*

Sheila: *You are obviously not happy with the situation, and the staff at Ridgeway House are also concerned. I am wondering if there is any way to help resolve the problem in a way that will help Jin. It seems that you and the staff are seeing Jin's position in Ridgeway House, and with the other children, in different ways. Maybe it might help to organise a meeting where these problems could be fully discussed. I am quite happy to be there if you think that might help.*

Mrs Chen: *I don't know. I would find it very hard to trust them again after all this but I know there is nowhere else for Jin to go. Please let me think about what you have said and talk about it with my husband.*

Sheila: *OK, well, if there's anything more you want to say?*

Mrs Chen: *No, thank you. You have been very helpful and I appreciate what you are doing. I will think about what you have said and I will let you know what my husband and I decide.*

Sheila: *Well, I hope the problem can be resolved and if there is anything I can do to help then that's my job.*

Mrs Chen: *Thank you very much for coming. I will give you a ring.*

Sheila: *Good-bye Mrs Chen.*

Mrs Chen: *Good-bye.*

Case sheet 4F, Children with physical and learning difficulties: Suggested record. Home visit to Mrs Chen

Mother: Mrs Chen
Worker: Sheila White
27th July 2000

Purpose of Visit: To discuss Mrs Chen's decision to withdraw her son Jin Chen from Ridgeway House Respite Unit, and her intention to make a complaint about the staff's care of her son.

I explained that I had just taken over the case but had read the file and talked to staff at Ridgeway House. I asked Mrs Chen if she could tell me about the situation from her perspective.

She recounted the incident six months ago when Jin was hit on the arm by another boy, saying the staff had phoned her when it happened but had told her there was nothing to worry about. She said she was shocked by the bruise two days later when she collected him and she said he seemed quieter than his usual self.

She was concerned about this change in Jin and two months later asked to speak to the manager of Ridgeway House. She felt her concerns had not been taken seriously with the manager saying that it was probably Jin's age and that he seemed OK and always had a good appetite. Mrs Chen was advised to speak to the key worker.

Mrs Chen felt the key worker was very young and not able to understand Jin. Mrs Chen was concerned that she did not know that Jin really enjoyed a bedtime story.

Her concerns grew when she called somewhat earlier to collect him in May and entered a room with the worker to find another boy poking and shouting at Jin. Mrs Chen said she thought Jin looked frightened. She did not feel the worker dealt with the situation adequately, telling the child to stop and then giving it something else to play with. Mrs Chen felt the child should have been told off and it should have been explained that it was not the right way to behave. She felt that even with their limited understanding the children should not be allowed to bully others. She said how her eldest son had been the victim of bullying, because of looking different. She was angry that the staff at Ridgeway House thought of it as no more than teasing.

She said that Jin had accompanied them on a family holiday in June but she had then decided not to send him back to the unit in July and she was going to make a formal complaint. She also said that she was worried about her own ability to cope alone with Jin, the problem of him becoming bored and the effect on her other children.

I suggested that it might help if a meeting were organised between her and some of the staff at Ridgeway House, which I would also attend in order to discuss the problem and try and find a resolution.

Mrs Chen said she wasn't sure she would be able to ever again trust the staff at Ridgeway House but she would think about my suggestion, discuss it with her husband and get back to me.

Training module: For the purpose of . . .

➚ Objective

The aim of this module is to illustrate how the different purposes of various records influence the way in which they are made. An incident is described in considerable detail on the case sheets. The information is then used by the learners to write both the entry in the accident book and the record in the client's personal file. The process requires learners to apply the principles of relevance, accuracy, completeness and conciseness in accordance with the purpose of the record. Once again, there are different versions for different learner groups, and for this exercise the case sheets come in two parts: a description of the incident and a suggested record.

🕐 Timing

Allow 45 minutes for this module.

✐ Materials

You will need:

- case sheets, *For the purpose of . . .*
  - 5A: Older people. Orchard Park Day Centre
  - 5B: Children and young people in residential care. Avalon House
  - 5C: Learning disability. Acorn Lodge
- paper
- pens

ⓘ Trainer's guidelines

Step 1: allow 5 minutes

Introduce the exercise and divide the participants into pairs. Distribute copies of the descriptive part of the appropriate case sheet and ask the learners to read them and then write two records of the incident, one for the accident book, and one for the personal file of the service user who was injured. It is advisable to allow the learners the option of either working together to produce both records, or working separately, one writing the entry for the accident book, and one the record for the personal file.

Step 2: allow 20 minutes

The participants take time to write the two records.

Step 3: allow 10 minutes

Ask each pair in turn to read out their version of the record for the accident book, and discuss with the group any discrepancies or variations in the accounts. Next, ask each pair to read out their version of the record in the personal file, and again discuss any discrepancies or variations in the accounts.

Step 4: allow 10 minutes

Give out copies of the suggested records for both the accident book and the personal file, and identify the main points in them. Draw out comparisons between the *suggested record*s and the participants' own records, by pointing up the main differences between the two different types of records. Remind the learners that the different purpose of the two records will determine the way in which each is made.

Case sheet 5A, Older people: For the purpose of . . . Orchard Park Day Centre

It was 8 May 2000. It was a beautiful morning and Reg, aged 79, was looking forward to going to the day centre. He had been on his own now for three years since his wife had died. She had been a lot older than him. His home carer had already been, and helped him to dress. He had felt like a cooked breakfast for a change, and she had done him some scrambled egg and toast. He had enjoyed that. Now he was just waiting for the bus to arrive.

Reg was soon on his way. He chatted to Cyril. They talked about the new manager at the centre and agreed that she seemed nice enough but they thought she was very young to be in charge. When they arrived, they went and sat down in the large lounge area and had coffee together. After coffee, they joined the exercise class run by Yvonne Roberts, who came to the centre every Wednesday. Reg and Cyril had both enjoyed sport when they were younger and welcomed the opportunity to be more physically active again.

Reg and Cyril took up their chairs. After about ten minutes of some gentle stretching exercises, Reg started to feel a little weak but he was determined to continue. Yvonne noticed he wasn't quite as lively as usual and asked if he wanted to rest but Reg told her not to fuss. The class finished after a little while. Reg was pleased that he had managed to get through it. It was not very long before lunch and so he joined in a game of dominoes with Cyril and Harry. It was nearly half past twelve and lunch would soon be ready so Reg decided to go to the toilet.

Reg went into the toilet cubicle and as he started to bend forward and undo his clothing he suddenly felt very strange and before he knew what was happening he had fallen against the toilet door. He ended up in a heap on the floor and could not get up. At first he was too shocked to say anything and then he started to call for help.

Iris, a careworker had told Harry and Cyril that lunch was ready. She asked where Reg had gone. They said he had gone to the toilet and so Iris went to look for him. As she approached the toilet she heard Reg calling out. She rushed in and asked what had happened. Reg explained through the toilet door that he had fallen. Iris said she would get Barbara, the manager. Barabara brought a key that opened the toilet doors from the other side. Carefully, Barbara and Iris opened the door; as they did so, Reg slid further forward until he was lying on the floor. He was still conscious but had a bruise and heavy bleeding from the right side of his head. He also complained that his right hip hurt. He seemed very shaken and distressed. Iris stayed with Reg while Barabara went to phone for an ambulance and to get the first aid box. She came back and washed the head wound with water and then applied a dressing, securing it with a bandage around

Reg's head. They did not move Reg but put cushions on the toilet floor around him, covering him with a blanket. Reg was very concerned that his neighbour, Mrs Wilkes, should be told about what had happened so she would look after his cat. After twenty minutes the ambulance arrived, checked for signs of a fracture but could not find any. They put him on a stretcher and took him to hospital. Barbara phoned Mrs Wilkes at 2.30 p.m.

Case sheet 5A, Older people: Suggested record. Orchard Park Day Centre

Accident book

Date: 8th May 2000
Time: approx. 12.35
Place: Toilets, Orchard Park Day Centre
Witnesses: Reg Taylor
Injury: Bleeding and Bruise to right side of head of Reg Taylor.
Pain in right hip.

Reg Taylor found in toilet by Iris Harris, calling for help from inside cubicle. Barbara Foster and Iris opened the cubicle to find Reg on the floor, with bruise and bleeding to the right side of his head. He was also complaining of pain in his right hip. Barbara phoned for ambulance and applied first aid, washing and dressing wound, securing dressing with bandage around the head. Reg was not moved. Cushions were placed around him and he was covered with a blanket. Ambulance arrived after twenty minutes and took Reg to hospital.

Reg's personal file

Reg had spent the morning in the exercise class. The instructor, Yvonne Roberts said that although he had appeared to find the exercises a little difficult this morning, he wanted to finish the class. Afterwards he played dominoes. Just before lunch he went to the toilet and was found a few minutes afterwards by Iris Harris, calling for help from inside the toilet cubicle. Barbara Foster and Iris opened the door and found Reg on the floor with a bruise and bleeding from the right side of his head. He was also complaining of pain in his right hip. He seemed very shaken and distressed. Barbara washed the head wound and applied dressing, secured with a bandage around the head. Reg was not moved and was covered with a blanket; cushions were placed around him to make him more comfortable. He was very concerned that his neighbour, Mrs Wilkes, be told about what had happened so that she would look after his cat. After twenty minutes the ambulance arrived and Reg was taken to hospital. Mrs Wilkes was phoned at 2.30 p.m.

Points for discussion

There is a question as to how much Reg's earlier difficulty in the exercise class was a warning that he was feeling unwell. This is relevant to the personal file but less relevant to the accident book. It could raise questions as to whether Reg should have been advised to not continue with the class and the possible liability of the instructor.

Case sheet 5B, Children and young people in residential care: For the purpose of . . . Avalon House

It was Monday 7th March 2000. Sophie, aged thirteen, was sitting in her room, playing a CD she had been given for her birthday. Sophie had not been feeling well that morning. It was that time of the month again and she always felt bad. She had argued with Lesley, a member of staff, over whether she should go to school or not. Lesley had said that she ought to make the effort. But Sophie didn't want to go to school. She didn't want to get up. She didn't want to do anything. She just felt bad. Finally, Lesley gave up and left Sophie in bed. Sophie slept for a bit and then she decided to play the CD.

Later on, Sophie heard Lesley come back upstairs and knock on her door. Lesley asked Sophie if she wanted any lunch. Sophie had not wanted any breakfast and so was beginning to feel quite hungry by now. She said she would come downstairs. It was one o'clock when she got down to the kitchen, Lesley was already beginning to prepare the lunch. She was cooking some pasta. Sophie liked pasta. Lesley asked what sauce Sophie wanted with it. Sophie rummaged through the cupboards and found a jar of tomato and something. She thought it looked OK and she vaguely remembered having it before. Lesley asked her to put it in the microwave and warm it up.

At that moment the phone rang. Lesley told Sophie the pasta wasn't quite cooked and would need another four minutes. Would she keep an eye on it, while Lesley was on the phone? Lesley went off to answer the phone. Sophie was really feeling hungry now. She tipped the sauce into bowl and put it into the microwave. She watched the pasta and then heard Lesley shout from the other room that she would be a few minutes sorting something out, and would Sophie turn the gas out. Sophie turned the gas out. After another couple of minutes the sauce was ready in the microwave. Sophie was getting fed up waiting for Lesley and so she decided to drain the pasta herself. She picked up the pan and took it over to the sink. She held the lid at an angle from the pan in the way she had seen her mother do. She didn't really know what happened next. All of a sudden the lid slipped out of her hand. She dropped the pan, and the boiling water and pasta splashed everywhere, over her hands and the lower part of her arms. She screamed in pain and shock. Lesley came rushing back into the kitchen and immediately turned on the cold water tap and told Sophie to hold her hands and arms under the running water.

Sophie was crying. The water was ice cold and seemed to be stinging as much as the boiling water. Lesley insisted Sophie keep her hands under the cold water for at least ten minutes. Sophie continued to sob. Lesley tried to reassure her and said that the cold water was really important to take the heat out of the scald. After ten minutes Lesley asked Sophie how it was feeling. Sophie said she couldn't feel anything, her hands had gone numb.

Lesley turned the tap off and carefully dried Sophie's hands with a clean towel. They were very red and there were two small blisters on her left hand. Lesley loosely wrapped Sophie's hands in sterile dressing and told her to sit quietly while she rang to check with the manager whether she should take Sophie to hospital.

Lesley was on her own in the home after Gillian, who was supposed to be working with her, was unable to come in that morning as her child had been rushed into hospital during the night. Lesley had been trying to get other staff to cover but without success. Lesley thought that she would probably be back from the hospital before the other young people came in from school, but she was worried that they might be delayed in casualty and someone might come home early from school. Lesley's manager asked how bad Sophie's scald was. Lesley said it was beginning to blister on one hand. Lesley's manager said she would come down to the home, while Lesley took Sophie to hospital. Half an hour later, Lesley accompanied Sophie to the hospital.

Case sheet 5B, Children and young people in residential care: Suggested record. Avalon House

Accident book

Date: 7th March 2000
Time: approx. 1.15 p.m.
Place: Kitchen at Avalon House
Witnesses: Lesley Carter and Sophie Ellis
Injury: Scald to both hands and lower arms of Sophie Ellis

Sophie Ellis was helping to prepare lunch in the kitchen with myself. I left the kitchen to answer the phone. I asked Sophie from the other room to turn the gas out on the pasta. After two minutes I heard Sophie cry out, rushed to the kitchen to find Sophie had spilled boiling water and pasta over her hands and lower arms while trying to strain them in the sink. She was screaming in pain. I told Sophie to hold her arms and hands under running cold water. After ten minutes I dried them with a clean towel. They were very red and there were two small blisters on her left hand. I wrapped her hands loosely in sterile dressing. When asked how she was feeling, Sophie said her hands had gone numb. As I was on my own in the unit, due to staff member unable to come in, and no other staff available, I phoned my manager who came to relieve me and thirty minutes later I took Sophie to the hospital.

Sophie's personal file

Sophie had spent the morning in bed, saying she felt too unwell to go to school, due to menstruation pains. Later in the morning I asked her if she wanted any lunch and she decided to come downstairs. She was helping me to prepare the pasta, warming the sauce in the microwave. I left the kitchen to answer the phone, asking Sophie to watch the pasta. After a couple of minutes I shouted to her to turn the gas out on the pasta. After another couple of minutes I heard a cry and rushed to the kitchen to find Sophie had spilled pasta and boiling water over her hands and lower arms while trying to strain the pasta. I immediately told her to hold her hands under cold running water. She was very upset, screaming and crying in pain, and complaining that the cold water was as painful as the hot. After ten minutes I dried her hands, which were very red, with two small blisters on the left hand, and wrapped them loosely in a sterile dressing. When asked how she was feeling, Sophie said her hands had gone numb. As I was on my own, I rang my manager about taking Sophie to hospital. My manager agreed to relieve me, and thirty minutes later I took Sophie to hospital.

Points for discussion

This incident raises questions about the reasonableness of leaving Sophie in the kitchen with the boiling pasta and asking her to turn the gas out. Could it be argued that Lesley had some responsibility in encouraging Sophie to lift the pan and take it to the sink to strain? The details around exactly what happened and what was said need to be carefully recorded.

There is also the question of the half an hour delay in taking her to hospital while Lesley checks with her manager about what she should do, because she is unsure how serious the injury is and she is on her own in the unit. It is important to know how Lesley came to be on her own. It is also relevant to know how Sophie was, after her hands had been covered, in evaluating the reasonableness of the delay.

Case sheet 5C, Learning disability: For the purpose of . . . Acorn Lodge

Derek is a resident at Acorn Lodge, a home for fifteen adults with learning disabilities. He was waiting on Sunday afternoon, 28th June 2000 for his brother, Laurie to arrive on his weekly visit. He was sitting in the garden as it was a lovely, hot, sunny day and he wanted to make the most of it. Geoff, his friend for many years, was sitting with him. They were chatting about the summer fete they had been to the previous afternoon.

At about 3.00 p.m. Laurie, Derek's brother, arrived with his new dog, Snout. Laurie had told Derek how he was going to get a new dog. His last one had died six months ago and he had said he wouldn't get another one, but in the end he missed the company and went along to the dog rescue centre to get another one.

Laurie was told that Snout, a terrier cross, had been badly treated, but he had such an intelligent look about him that Laurie decided, as soon as he saw him, that that was the dog for him. Laurie brought Snout around to the garden where Derek and Geoff were sitting. Snout got a bit excitable and ran up to Derek, jumping up at him and trying to lick him. Derek rubbed his ears and patted his head.

Geoff had always been very fond of dogs and said he wanted to play with Snout. Laurie explained that he was still training Snout and it was best if Geoff didn't get him too excited. Geoff found a stick and started throwing it for Snout to run and fetch. Geoff then started to hold the stick above his head and encouraged Snout to jump and try and get it. Laurie again warned Geoff that Snout was getting too excited. Snout was jumping higher and higher and getting more frustrated that he couldn't get the stick. Geoff was laughing and trying to hide the stick from the dog. As Geoff waved the stick above the dog, Snout made a huge leap and attempted to get the stick. Geoff moved his hand sharply and Snout caught his right hand. Geoff shouted that the dog had bitten him, and showed Laurie and Derek the teeth marks which had drawn blood.

Laurie was angry, and said that it was Geoff's fault and that he had warned him several times not to get the dog over excited. Derek was concerned for his friend, but agreed with his brother that Geoff was more to blame than the dog. Geoff was in pain from the bite and angry that Derek and Laurie were saying it was his fault. He went to find Hilary, the senior staff on duty, to tell her what had happened.

Hilary washed and dressed Geoff's wound, and then checked his records to make sure his tetanus injection was up to date. There was no record, so she arranged for Kevin, a care worker, to go with him to casualty to have it done.

She talked to Laurie and Derek about the incident. Laurie was still angry about Geoff and said he had told the dog off but it wasn't really Snout's fault anyway. He had warned Geoff enough times but he had taken no notice. Derek became very anxious when he heard Geoff had gone to hospital. Hilary explained that it was just a precaution and that Geoff was all right and would be home soon.

Case sheet 5C, Learning disability: Suggested record. Acorn Lodge

Accident book

Date: 28th June 2000
Time: approx. 3.15 p.m.
Place: Garden at Acorn Lodge
Witnesses: Geoff Murray, Derek Hinton and Laurie Hinton
Injury: Bite mark to right hand of Geoff Murray

Geoff Murray was playing with a dog brought into the garden by Laurie Hinton, while visiting his brother, Derek Hinton. Laurie claimed that he warned Geoff several times not to get the dog over-excited. This was confirmed by Derek. Geoff continued to encourage the dog to jump for a stick he was holding. As the dog jumped, it bit Geoff's right hand.

I washed and dressed the wound and after finding no record of an up-to-date tetanus injection, sent Geoff, with Kevin as escort, to casualty for injection.

Geoff's personal file

While Geoff was in the garden with another resident, who is his friend, they were joined by the friend's brother and his dog. Geoff started to play with the dog. According to the brother and the resident, the brother warned Geoff not to get the dog over-excited. Geoff continued to play with the dog, encouraging it to jump for a stick. As the dog jumped it bit Geoff's right hand.

Geoff came to seek assistance at about 3.15 p.m. He said the dog had bitten him, and he was angry because his friend and his friend's brother had blamed him for what had happened. Geoff was just having some fun with the dog and he was upset when the dog bit him.

I washed and dressed the wound and sent Geoff, with Kevin as escort, to casualty for tetanus injection after I found no record of an up-to-date injection.

Points for discussion

This is a potentially serious issue where there may well be questions of liability. Should the unit have allowed Laurie to bring the dog on the premises? Should Laurie be held responsible for the behaviour of his dog, even though Geoff ignored his warnings? The matter could conceivably result in the dog having to be put down. It may be advisable to also note in Derek's file that he was worried on hearing that his friend had gone to hospital and had been reassured that his friend had gone for a routine injection.

Training module: Your witness . . . making a record from role-play

↗ Objective

The aim of this module is to demonstrate the difficulties of accurately observing an incident and of providing a reliable and factual account of that observation. The case sheet material provides scenarios for two or three participants to use role-play, usually involving a dramatic or violent incident. The other course participants are then asked to write an eyewitness account of what they have observed. The comparison of these accounts and the accompanying discussion illustrate the very variable way in which people both observe, recollect and then describe incidents which they have witnessed. The exercise emphasises the importance of making a factual record, while at the same time allowing learners to appreciate that their perception of the facts is not always as reliable or as accurate as they might sometimes assume. Again, there are different versions of the case sheets for different learner groups.

⏱ Timing

Allow 50 minutes, though timings are particularly approximate in this module.

✎ Materials

You will need:

- case sheets, *Your witness . . . making a record from role-play*
  - 6A: Older people in residential care. Larkland Grove
  - 6B: Children and young people in residential care. Larchwood House
  - 6C: Learning disability in residential care. Forsythia House
  - 6D: Mental health. Silverside Day Centre
- flipchart and markers
- paper
- pens
- certain additional props will be needed for some of the scenarios, see individual case sheets

ⓘ Trainer's guidelines

Step 1: allow approximately 10 minutes

Introduce the exercise by explaining briefly what is to happen, and ask for volunteers for the role-play; some of the group are going to act and some are going to record. You may get a more enthusiastic response, if you point out as an incentive that the volunteer actors will not have to write the eyewitness account! Take the actors into a separate room and brief them on what they are going to do. Give them the appropriate case sheet and allow them time to select their roles and briefly prepare themselves. Back with the rest of the group, brief the observers, who are going to record, about the setting and characters involved in the storyline. Ask them not to make any notes during the role-play, explaining that after it is finished, they will be expected to write, individually, an eyewitness account of the incident they have just observed. Arrange whatever props are needed in the main room where the observers are.

Step 2: allow 10 minutes

The actors act out the storyline from the case sheet, in the main room, in front of the observers. You may need to set a maximum time limit for the acting, as although this part often takes no more than five minutes, some participants have been known to keep going for longer.

Step 3: allow 10 minutes

After the actors have finished and are taking a break, ask the observers to write their eyewitness accounts. It may be advisable, while the observers are writing, to spend a few minutes with the actors in a separate room, helping them to 'de-role'. Most participants will approach the exercise very light-heartedly, but if there is any suggestion that the role players are experiencing difficulty as a consequence of their participation in the role-play, they may need some support. Ask them how they felt during the role-play, and how they are feeling now, and help them to distinguish the character from themselves.

Step 4: allow 10 minutes

Divide the observers into groups of three or four, and ask them to read out their individual accounts to one another. You and the actors should now wander between the groups and listen in on the different accounts, though you should warn the observers before you do so. Explain that the objective is not necessarily to identify the best account, but to compare the different records with one another and with the actors' recollections of what happened.

Step 5: allow 10 minutes

Ask the actors to discuss with the group, their responses to the observers' accounts, and how they compare with their own recollections of the incident. Allow the observers to make further reflections, now they have listened to each other's accounts. Draw out any discrepancies and emphasise the important points arising from each storyline: each case sheet contains *Points for the Record* to help with this.

Case sheet 6A, Older people in residential care: Your witness . . . Larkland Grove

Role play for three people

Props: chair and walking stick
Scene: communal area in a residential home for older people
Characters: Dorothy, Jack and Carol

Dorothy

You are staying at Larkland Grove for the first time, on a respite visit, and are considering whether to accept a permanent place.

You are sitting in a chair by the window, enjoying the view, when Jack, a gentleman, who seemed rather confused when you saw him earlier in the dining room, approaches you and starts shouting that you are in his chair.

You feel quite frightened but don't see why Jack has any more right to the chair than you do. Anyway, you object to his rudeness. You continue to sit in the chair despite his increasingly abusive language.

When Carol arrives, you start crying and say that you don't want to ever come to the home again. You've never been so upset. You start to complain that you feel unwell, and by the end of the incident are experiencing very real difficulty in breathing.

Jack

You have lived in Larkland Grove for over five years, and although you miss your own garden and sometimes feel a little confused, you have settled in fairly well. You like a particular chair which provides a good view of the garden. Today you find someone you've never seen before sitting in the chair. You shout at her that it's your chair but she refuses to move. You get increasingly angry and start swearing, calling the woman a 'fucking cow'. You start to bang the legs of the chair with your stick.

When Carol arrives you expect her to sort the woman out, but when you don't seem to be getting your chair back, you lose your temper and lunge at Carol with your stick, miss and fall over. You feel a sharp pain in your leg and cry out.

Carol

You are a relatively inexperienced, new, care assistant, who has heard shouting. Following the noise, you find Dorothy and Jack arguing over the chair. You try to calm the situation down. Dorothy just starts crying and says she feels unwell. Jack gets more angry, lunges at you with his stick, you put your arm up to protect yourself, Jack misses and falls over. Jack appears to be in pain with his leg.

N.B. It is important when Jack raises his stick to Carol and she puts up her arm to defend herself, that the arm and stick do not make contact but look as though they might have done.

Points for the record

1. Did the observers note Jack's actual actions and words or did they just describe him as being aggressive and verbally abusive?
2. Did the observers describe how Dorothy was having difficulty in breathing by the end of the incident? This very often gets overlooked in all the commotion between Carol and Jack.
3. Did the observers make judgmental statements about Carol's handling of the situation, rather than keeping to a factual description of what she did, and what happened?
4. How much detail were they able to provide about the most critical moment in the incident, when Jack raised his stick and fell? Did observers implicate Carol in contributing to Jack falling over? This is a potentially very serious point in the incident and needs to be described very carefully. Observers' descriptions may well be influenced by their vantage point in relation to the action. How much were they able to see? How much were they able to remember?

Case sheet 6B, Children and young people in residential care: Your witness . . . Larchwood House

Role play for three people

Props: chair and radiator or something to simulate one, e.g. table
Scene: living room in a residential home for young people
Characters: Erica, Stacey and Gary

Erica

You have had a bath earlier in the evening and accidentally left your watch behind in the bathroom. The watch was a gift from your grandmother last Christmas. You realised that you had left the watch in the bathroom after Stacey had come out after her bath. You went to search the bathroom but could not find the watch.

You join Stacey in the living room and ask her what she's done with your watch. When Stacey says she didn't see any watch, you accuse her of lying, and say that she must have taken the watch, as there is no sign of it now. You have never liked Stacey. She always seemed rather sneaky to you. You start to insult Stacey, saying that just because Stacey hasn't got any friends she has to start taking other people's things. You become angrier and accuse Stacey of stealing your watch.

At this point, you are joined by Gary, an inexperienced member of staff who tries to calm the situation down, but Stacey becomes angry, and tells you to shut up, pushing you out of the way as she leaves the room, which causes you to fall against the hot radiator and cry out in pain.

Stacey

You have just finished your bath and gone into the living room where you are sitting down about to watch some TV. Erica comes in asking you what you've done with her watch. You don't remember seeing any watch and don't know what Erica is going on about. When she accuses you of stealing the watch because you have few friends, you become very angry. You have never really liked Erica. You think she is too loud, and believe she has it in for you. You were often accused of stealing things at home.

When Gary comes into the room and tries to calm things down, you just feel you have had enough and want to go back to your room. You are now close to tears and rush out of the door pushing past Erica who is in the way.

Gary

You are an inexperienced member of care staff who hears shouting in the living room, and when you find Erica and Stacey arguing, you try to calm things down. The two girls ignore you and you are not sure how to handle the situation. Stacey gets up and rushes from the room pushing Erica against the radiator as she leaves.

Points for the record

1. Did the observers note the girls' actual actions and words or did they just describe them as being aggressive and verbally abusive? Did they try to apportion blame between the girls or did they keep to an impartial description of what took place?
2. Did the observers make judgmental statements about Gary's handling of the situation rather than keeping to a factual description of what he did and what happened?
3. How much detail were they able to provide about the critical moment in the incident when Stacey rushed from the room, knocking Erica against the hot radiator? Did they presume the action had been intentional on Stacey's part or did they describe it as an accident? An eye witness cannot always be sure about motives and needs to keep to a factual description of the behaviour they actually observed.

Case sheet 6C, Learning disability in residential care: Your witness . . . Forsythia House

Role play for three people

Props: low table, TV or a box to simulate one, chair and plastic cup
Scene: living room in a residential home
Characters: Joe, Allison and Vanessa

Joe

You are 29 years old and have been living at Forsythia House for three years. It is 11 o'clock on a Saturday morning and you are sitting, watching TV. You were supposed to be going into town with Vanessa, a support worker, to buy your Gran a birthday present, but it is raining and you don't fancy going out yet. You are enjoying your programme, when Allison comes in and says she wants to change the channel to another programme. Allison has lived in the house for three months and you feel she just wants her own way all the time. You refuse. You and Allison start to argue, and shout at one another.

You are joined by Vanessa, who reminds you that you were meant to go shopping with her. You are determined not to give way to Allison and you don't want to go out in the rain. You tell both of them to leave you alone.

When Allison tries to change the channel, you attempt to stop her. At that point she spills the hot coffee she is carrying and you cry out in pain.

Allison

You are aged 22 and have been living at Forsythia House for three months. You have found it difficult to settle in. Everyone seems boring and you are fed up. It is Saturday morning and there is a particular TV programme you wanted to watch. You did have a TV in your room but it is not working and it will be a week before it is fixed.

You find Joe in the living room. You ask if you can change channels. Joe refuses. You become impatient and feel that Joe is just doing it to upset you. You start to argue. Vanessa comes into the room, and when she reminds Joe he was supposed to go into town with her to buy his Gran's birthday present, you feel you should be allowed to watch your programme. Joe still refuses. As you become more angry, calling Joe a 'fucking wanker', Vanessa warns you to be careful not to spill the hot cup of coffee you are carrying. You shout at Vanessa that if she can't do anything about it then you'll sort it yourself. You go to switch the channel but Joe tries to stop you and in the struggle you spill the coffee over him.

Vanessa

You are a relatively inexperienced member of care staff who has worked at the house for six months. You had arranged to go shopping with Joe to get his Gran's birthday present. You go to find him and then hear him shouting with Allison in the living room. They are arguing over the TV. You try to persuade Joe to come shopping. He refuses and Allison becomes more angry. You warn Allison to be careful not to spill the coffee. She continues to insist that she be allowed to watch her programme. You try to calm the situation down but Allison attempts to change the channel. Joe tries to stop her, at which point Allison spills the coffee over Joe.

Points for the record

1. Did the observers note Joe and Allison's actual actions and words, or did they just describe them as being aggressive and verbally abusive? Did they try to apportion blame or did they keep to a factual description of what took place?
2. Did the observers make judgmental statements about Vanessa's handling of the situation rather than keeping to a factual description of what she did and said?
3. How much detail were they able to provide about the critical moment in the incident, when Allison tried to change the TV channel, Joe tried to stop her, and Allison spilled the coffee over Joe? Did they presume the action had been intentional on Allison's part or did they describe it as an accident? An eye witness cannot always be sure about motives and needs to keep to a factual description of the behaviour they actually observed.

Case sheet 6D, Mental health: Your witness . . . Silverside Day Centre

Role play for three people

Props: two tables and two cardboard boxes to simulate computers
Scene: computer room
Characters: Peter, Sheila and George

Peter

Peter is a young man who has been suffering from acute anxiety and depression since he was 19. His problems started when he went away to university. He was unable to continue and left at the end of his first year. Since then he has been receiving treatment and has been making progress. He has now decided to attend a basic course in using computers at the local day centre he attends.

Peter is trying to complete an exercise but he is finding it very difficult. He still has problems concentrating. He dislikes Sheila and finds her constant complaining to George about not being able to do things and not understanding his instructions very irritating. He thinks she's just trying to flirt with George. He feels frustrated with himself and with Sheila. He tells Sheila to shut up because he can't hear himself think. When she responds angrily, he feels even more agitated and unable to handle the situation. He then accuses Sheila of not giving a damn about anybody else except herself. He tells her she's just a 'selfish, attention-seeking bitch'. After Sheila throws the book at him, he rushes from the room, shoving against the table and knocking his computer to the floor, pushing George out of his way as he runs out.

Sheila

Sheila is a woman in her early twenties who has suffered from anorexia since she was a teenager. She appears to be responding well to treatment and is now following a course in computer skills at the day centre she attends.

Sheila finds the work difficult and feels the need to keep checking with George what she should be doing. She also rather likes George and wants him to notice her. She reacts angrily when Peter tells her to shut up. As the argument continues she becomes more and more excited, accusing Peter of being a 'pathetic bastard'. Finally she screams at him to 'Fuck off!' and throws a book at him. As he rushes out, she shouts after him 'Stupid wanker!'

George

George is a relatively inexperienced worker at the day centre. He was appointed to help set up the programme in computer skills. George tries to intervene in the argument but is unable to calm the situation. George has difficulty in maintaining his balance when Peter rushes past him and falls over the computer which is now on the floor.

Points for the record

1. How far did the observers note the actual actions and words used, or did they just describe people as being aggressive and verbally abusive?
2. Did the observers try to apportion blame as to who was responsible for the incident, rather than sticking to a factual description?
3. Did the observers make judgmental statements about George's competence in handling the incident or did they keep to a factual description of what he did and what happened?
4. How much detail were the observers able to provide about the most critical moment in the incident, when Sheila throws the book and Peter gets up and rushes from the room, pushing the computer to the floor and thereby causing George to fall over the computer? This is a serious point in the incident and needs to be described carefully. Observers' descriptions may well be influenced by their vantage point in relation to the action. How much were they able to see? How much were they able to remember?

Section 7: Advanced Training Modules

Training module: The record as evidence

↗ Objective

The aim of this module is to recognise the implications of an incident and to understand the significance of the record as evidence. Learners are asked to read an account of a service user's day, during which an incident occurs, although exactly what happened is unclear. When recording the participants need to be aware of the possible implications of the incident and bear in mind the importance of their record as possible evidence. Again the exercise is worked from a case sheet, although this time there is only one version; it has a similar storyline to that in *Making a Record from Transcripts: Jane Gillespie*.

🕐 Timing

Allow 45 minutes for this module.

✏ Materials

You will need:

- case sheet 7: *The record as evidence*, learning disability
- paper
- pens

ⓘ Trainer's guidelines

Step 1: allow 30 minutes

Introduce and briefly describe the exercise, and divide the participants into groups of three or four. Distribute the case sheet, before asking the participants to write Veronica's record of Jane's day.

Step 2: allow 15 minutes

Ask each group to read aloud their version of the record, and then review the different records in terms of:

1. How far did the record give a brief picture of Jane before she went to the day centre? This may be relevant in establishing Jane's mood before she left it, and returned to the home.
2. What happened on the way back from the centre? It will be important to have a picture of Jane after the incident.
3. How much detail was provided of Jane describing what happened? Were there verbatim quotes? Were there descriptions of Jane's behaviour? This is the most crucial point in the whole exchange between Veronica and Jane.
4. Was there a short description of what Jane did after describing the incident?

It is not clear from the account what has happened. The incident may be something Jane has made up, because she does not want to go to the centre, or she may have been indecently assaulted by Robert, or perhaps something in between those two extremes. When making the record, it is important to recognise the serious implications of such an incident, and to record in as much detail as possible, anything that will help to establish exactly what happened.

Case sheet 7, The record as evidence. Learning disability: Jane

Jane is a 29-year-old woman with learning disability. She is a new resident at the home after recently losing her mother, who had looked after her all her life. Jane's father had died when she was thirteen. She came to the home a week ago and at first was rather withdrawn. She has slowly started to talk with more people and has made friends with several other residents.

On Monday 26th August Jane awoke to the sounds of people outside her room. She heard Veronica, one of the members of staff, talking to her new friend Vicky. She still wasn't used to getting up this early. With her mother, things had been more relaxed in the morning. She wanted the toilet so decided to get up. She was a little apprehensive about going to the new centre. She had been used to going to one near to where her mother lived, but the move into the home had made a change necessary.

Veronica greeted Jane as she emerged from her room and headed towards the toilet. Jane responded with a smile and Veronica was pleased to see her more at ease with people. As Jane went back to her room, Veronica reminded her that she hadn't long before breakfast and offered to help her get ready. Jane still found it difficult to get herself organised in the morning, as she had been heavily reliant on her mother for so many years.

Veronica chatted about how much she liked Jane's new hair-cut, while Jane brushed her teeth and washed her face. They talked about how Jane was feeling about going to the new centre for the first time. Veronica encouraged Jane to think positively, although was quite surprised to see that Jane was already much less nervous than she had anticipated. They then selected some clean trousers and a T-shirt for Jane to wear. Jane was not used to making decisions for herself and needed encouragement. They walked down to breakfast. On the way they ran into Vicky. Jane and Vicky started to talk about the previous day when they had gone out on a special trip to Bournemouth. They had really enjoyed going into the sea and particularly liked the fun fair rides.

When they got to the dining room, they sat together with two other residents, Annie and Melanie. Veronica went off to ask Dave, another resident, to help serve the breakfasts.

Jane didn't really like the food at the home. She preferred her Mum's cooking and missed the way she would fuss over her in the morning, cooking her a full breakfast. People told her it was better for her not to eat so much fatty food and that she needed to cut down. Jane ate the scrambled eggs put before her, but she would have liked the bacon, sausages and mushrooms she would have had with Mum.

Veronica was pleased to see that Jane was now eating well and had finished all of her breakfast. When she first arrived she had shown little interest in the food put before her. Veronica observed that Jane appeared to be much more involved in the conversation going on at her table, frequently laughing and giggling at what was being said by the others.

After breakfast, Veronica checked with Jane that she had all she needed for her first day. The bus would be picking them up in about 15 minutes and Jane was beginning to get quite nervously excited. Veronica reassured her that everything would be fine and that she would soon settle in and make new friends, just as she was doing in the home. Vicky joined them in the lounge and they got on the bus together when it finally arrived.

At about 11.30 Marilyn, the senior member of staff on duty, received a call from the centre. It seemed that Jane had become very upset following an incident with Robert, attending the centre from another residential home. It was not entirely clear what had happened, but Jane claimed that Robert had tried to follow her into the toilet and had said rude things to her and then tried to grab her, although she was too upset to give a very clear account of what had actually taken place. Robert had become very angry when he was asked what had happened and said Jane was just telling lies because she didn't like him. It was decided that it would be better to collect Jane from the centre and bring her back to the home.

Veronica drove to the centre, and found a very tearful Jane, who clearly wanted to go home as soon as possible. On the way back in the car, Veronica tried to gently find out a little more about what had happened but Jane only continued to repeat that she didn't like Robert and didn't want to go back to the centre ever again.

On arrival back at the home, Jane wanted to go to her room. Veronica stayed with her and continued to try and comfort her. Eventually Jane became quieter and calmer but now seemed embarrassed to talk about the incident with Robert. Veronica decided that there was little point in pursuing the matter at this time. Jane was clearly reluctant to say anything more and pressing her would only upset her still further. Veronica suggested that she might like something to eat as it was lunch time, and she had missed out on anything to eat at the centre. Jane visibly brightened and they went into the kitchen and prepared a meal together. Veronica asked Jane what she would like and Jane opted for burger and chips with baked beans. She enjoyed cooking the meal with Veronica and said a little more about the centre while they were eating.

Jane indicated that she had liked working in the greenhouse. This was something she had done in her other centre. She had been helping to pot up some seedlings. Robert had also been working in the greenhouse. He had seemed very friendly and Jane had quite liked him. She thought he was funny and she had laughed at his jokes but she didn't know what to do when he followed her into the toilet. She had told him to go out but he wouldn't go and started to say how he thought she was really pretty and he wanted to kiss her. Jane became more uncomfortable as she was recalling the events of earlier on, and was unwilling to say very much more. She looked at the table while she was talking and repeatedly clasped and unclasped her hands. Veronica tried to press her a little more but Jane only became subdued and withdrawn.

After lunch Veronica suggested Jane might like to watch some television. Jane agreed to the idea and soon became engrossed in the day's episode of Neighbours. *Veronica meanwhile went to speak with the senior staff on duty and tell her what Jane had said over lunch. Veronica then returned to Jane and explained that she would shortly be going off duty but the others would be coming back from the centre before too long. Jane seemed very reserved and said she wanted to return to her room and look at a magazine.*

Training module: Assessing needs from role-play

↗ Objective

The aim of this module is to apply the principles of good recording practice in an assessment situation, ensuring an accurate account of the service user's perspective together with an identification of the relevant issues. Learners are asked to observe a role-play between a service user and a worker, and record the discussion between them before writing an Assessment Report, detailing recommended action. Where care managers are using an assessment process that incorporates the two stages into one document, the exercise can be adapted accordingly. There are, as before, different versions for different client groups.

🕐 Timing

Allow 1 hour 15 minutes for this module.

✏ Materials

You will need:

- case sheets, *Assessing needs*:
    - 8A: Older people. Bill and Emily Watson
    - 8B: Children and young people. Heidi and Andrew Webb
    - 8C: Physical disability. Irma Grosse
- paper
- pens

ⓘ Trainer's guidelines

Step 1: allow 10 minutes

Briefly introduce the exercise to the group and ask for two volunteers to be actors in the role-play. Again, you may get more willing volunteers, if they realise that those who don't act will be observing and making the record. Give out the appropriate case sheet to all the participants, including the observers. Allow the actors a few minutes to familiarise themselves with their characters and situation, while you are dividing the rest of the group into pairs.

Step 2: allow 10-15 minutes

The actors act out the storyline on the case sheet, while the rest of the group watch.

Step 3: allow 10 minutes

The pairs of observers now record the discussion they have just observed, as if they were the worker.

Step 4: allow 15 minutes

All the participants, including the actors, now work in pairs to produce the Assessment Report.

Step 5: allow 15 minutes

Each pair reads out their report. The trainer by drawing out relevant observations from the group should evaluate the reports, according to how far they:

- Applied the principles of good recording practice.
- Identified the main issues.
- Included the service user's perspective, even if the final conclusion is not necessarily in complete agreement with what the service user wanted.
- Made a clear statement of the recommendations and the reasons why they were being made.

Case sheet 8A, Older people: Assessing needs. Bill and Emily Watson

Background

Emily Watson is 85 years old and has lived with her husband Bill, aged 83, for the past sixty years. They own their three bedroom terraced house, where they have lived for thirty six years. They had three children, who all married, although their eldest son died five years ago of a heart attack. There are eight grandchildren, who are all in their late teens and twenties. Of the two remaining children, Sandra lives in the United States and Edward lives in Scotland. Sandra visits every few years and Edward tries to visit at least three times a year. Their widowed daughter-in-law has not been in good health since the death of her husband and they have seen little of her recently. Emily and Bill used to go and stay with their children but they have found the travelling too tiring in the last few years.

Emily and Bill used to run a small post office and general store together. They have enjoyed a close and companionable marriage, sharing various interests and hobbies. They loved ballroom dancing and were regional champions for several years. They were also active in local politics and Bill was a councillor for ten years.

They have both become more frail in recent years, although still fiercely independent. Bill had a small stroke twelve months ago and now needs a frame to get around. Despite some initial reluctance, they have been receiving domiciliary care support since Bill's stroke. They have both built up very positive relationships with their care workers.

Emily has been in hospital for the past six weeks after a serious fall, when she fractured her hip. Emily has deteriorated quite seriously since the accident, developing chest complications and appearing increasingly confused as to where she is and what has happened to her. The doctors are agreed that Emily will require nursing care for some time, if not permanently.

Bill has been very distressed by his wife's accident. He has been taken to visit her twice a week by volunteers. Both Sandra and Edward have visited in the last six weeks and are very worried about how their father will manage on his own. Neither of them have the room to have him live with them. Both of them still have grown up children living at home. Bill does not want to leave the area. He misses his wife and wants to be as near to her as he can, although he has become very upset at her confusion. Bill has not been eating properly during the last six weeks and is very dependent on someone to organise his domestic routine, relying heavily on his children or the home care workers who have been calling in more frequently.

Last week Bill was on his own trying to make a cup of tea for himself. As he was lifting the kettle, his hand trembled and the kettle slipped from his grasp, spilling boiling water over his other hand and legs. Despite the shock, Bill was able to call for help and is now, himself, in hospital, although not the same one as his wife. He is very anxious and depressed, feeling the accident was his fault, that he should have been more careful and that he has let his wife down as he is no longer able to visit her.

Role-play between Bill Watson and the Care Manager, to discuss Bill's future needs

Bill Watson

You are in hospital, being visited by Adrian, the new social worker who has been assigned to you. You are very worried about what is going to happen to you, and your wife. You are especially upset that you have not been able to visit her since you came into hospital. You want to return home with your wife.

Care Manager

The purpose of the visit is to discuss the care options available to Bill in the future. You are concerned to identify Bill's needs and then discuss with Emily's care manager what implications her situation may have for Bill.

Case sheet 8B, Children and young people: Assessing needs. Heidi and Andrew Webb

Background

Heidi (aged ten) and Andrew Webb (aged thirteen) are sister and brother and have been staying at Belmont Avenue care home for six children for the past eight months after their mother abandoned them. Mrs Webb first came to the attention of social services eight years ago when Heidi was put on the At Risk Register after Heidi was admitted to hospital with a fractured arm and bruises. Mrs Webb eventually disclosed that her current boy friend was responsible, saying he was under a lot of pressure after having lost his job. The relationship soon ended but successive relationships continued to cause concern over the children's welfare.

Mrs Webb has been treated for depression for the last two years and twelve months ago the situation deteriorated further, when she began a new relationship with a man who had previous convictions for sexual abuse of children. When informed that the man constituted a risk to her children, Mrs Webb refused to discuss the matter. Shortly after, she asked for the children to be put into care, left her current address and is believed to be with the man in question. The children were accommodated under section 20 of the Children Act. There have been intermittent phone calls (four in all) from her to the children during the last eight months and she sent cards and presents on their birthdays and at Christmas. The phone calls have been emotional with Mrs Webb often crying, saying how much she loves them and how she is sorry she can't look after them. Attempts to make contact with Mrs Webb have been unsuccessful and even when she phones the home, staff have been unable to discuss with her plans for the children's future.

The children are finding it increasingly difficult to cope with the present situation. Both become very distressed after talking to their mother. Heidi has become very withdrawn and finds it difficult to mix with other children in the home except her brother, with whom she remains very close. She has speech problems which do not seem to be improving despite the intervention of a speech therapist. She is struggling at school and has a reading age of six. When asked, Heidi has said that she would like to live with a foster family but she does not want to be parted from her brother.

Andrew is adamant he does not want to join a foster family, nor does he want to be separated from Heidi. He is convinced his mother will return and take them home. He remains very protective and affectionate toward his sister and has been involved with fights with other children in the home when he believes they have been teasing her because of her speech problems. Andrew has been excluded from one school for fighting. He started at West Dean Comprehensive, two months after coming to the home and already there have been three suspensions due to fighting. The school is concerned to support Andrew but feel that, if his behaviour does not improve, it will only be a matter of time before they will also have to exclude him. Andrew admits that he easily loses his temper and becomes violent but feels that he is provoked and gets blamed because of his reputation. He wants very much to be given a chance and has shown ability when he makes the effort, but his performance is not consistent. Despite attempts by staff in the home to help Andrew with these problems, his violent behaviour, involving damage to property and injury to other children, remains a serious cause of concern.

Role-play between Andrew and the Key Worker or Care Manager to discuss the options for Andrew's future

Key Worker or Care Manager

You have arranged to discuss with Andrew the options for his future, including the possibility of foster care, while also making him aware that his sister's future is also being considered and it may not be possible to keep them together.

There has been a general agreement by those involved in working with Heidi that her need for a stable family environment is now so acute that separate fostering may have to go ahead, although there are concerns about the effect that splitting up the brother and sister would have on them both. Whatever arrangements are made it is felt that it would be important for Heidi and Andrew to maintain contact through regular visits.

Andrew

You are very anxious about what the authorities might be planning. You are sure your Mum will come back for you and Heidi, but you are worried that if your Mum heard you had gone into foster care, she might feel that you didn't want her anymore and you would never see her again. You believe it is important you and Heidi stay together and Heidi needs you to look after her.

Case sheet 8C, Physical disability: Assessing needs. Irma Grosse

Background

Irma Grosse is a 28-year-old woman who has been blind from birth. Her mother is English and her father is German. Five years ago she was in a road traffic accident and suffered injuries to her spine. Since then she has used a wheelchair. Before the accident, Irma had been living with her parents. She felt that her parents' house was unsuitable for a wheelchair and she wanted greater independence. Irma was then offered a specially adapted council flat. Two years ago she began a relationship with Jerry. Despite her disabilities, Irma very much wanted a family and nine months ago she gave birth to a baby boy. Since the birth, they have received support from social services, in the form of a family aide, to help with the care of the baby and to monitor the situation. While Jerry was at first very involved with the baby, there have been increasing tensions and difficulties between him and Irma. Jerry had started a new job and was finding it difficult. He had complained to the family aide that Irma didn't seem to be interested in him anymore and only cared about the baby. Two weeks ago he left the home and although there have been several phone calls, there are no plans at the moment for him to return. Irma is saying that she is not sure that she wants him back anyway.

Since Jerry's departure there have been increasing concerns about Irma's ability to manage with the baby. She is very determined that the baby remains with her with additional input from social services. The family aide feels that Irma wants the baby but has relied so much on other people, especially Jerry, that she now underestimates what is involved in looking after the child. The family aide says that she feels under increasing strain in the situation as she thinks Irma expects her to do everything that Jerry used to do. In addition, as the baby grows older, he is becoming more active and is becoming fretful at being left for long periods in his cot. The family aide has pointed out to Irma that he needs to be given the opportunity to play; Irma usually responds by getting angry and upset and claiming that the family aide is trying to say she's a bad mother.

In addition you have been approached by the health visitor who is also feeling frustrated in her attempts to talk with Irma about the baby's needs. She reports that the baby has not gained any weight in the last month, has had a runny nose and was crying for most of the time during her last two visits.

**Role-play between Irma Grosse and Care Manager to discuss the
support needed for her and the baby.**

Care Manager

You are concerned that reports from the family aide and health visitor are
suggesting that, following the departure of Irma's partner, Jerry, Irma now
requires a much higher level of support. You are visiting her at home to
review the situation, to share the concerns of the family aide and health
visitor, and to assess what is needed, while also considering the resource
implications of any increased care package.

Irma Grosse

You are extremely anxious about any suggestions that you cannot cope
with your baby now that your partner, Jerry has left. You are determined
to bring the baby up, as a single parent if necessary, and you feel social
services should provide the level of support you need.

Section 8: Management Skills Training Modules

Training module: Writing a disciplinary report

↗ Objective

The aim of this module is to apply the principles of accuracy, relevance, conciseness and completeness in relation to the production of management reports. Learners are asked to review documentary evidence from those involved in, or who were witness to an incident in a residential unit, and to write a report of the incident, including recommendations for further action.

🕐 Timing

Allow one hour for this module.

✏️ Materials

You will need:

- case sheet 9, *Writing a disciplinary report: statements by observers*
- paper
- pens
- access to photocopier while the module is in progress

ⓘ Trainer's guidelines

Step 1: allow 40 minutes

Introduce the exercise by briefly explaining how it will work, hand out copies of case sheet 9, and divide the participants into groups of three or four. Each group will assume the position of the home manager, and use details on the case sheet to produce a report on the incident for the home manager's supervisor. The report should include recommendations for further action, such as disciplinary proceedings. When each group has finished their report, the trainer arranges for each of the reports to be copied, so they can be shared with the other groups.

Step 2: allow 20 minutes

Each group presents their report and the trainer draw out comparisons, and highlights the important issues:

1. Is there a clear statement as to the purpose of the report?
2. Is there a brief description of the incident which outlines the main events, the individuals involved and the witnesses, e.g.:
   - the disturbance in the lounge
   - Brian and Judy being called into the office by Sophie
   - Brian leaving the unit?

3. Does the report highlight the aspects of the incident which are corroborated, and those where there are discrepancies or differences over interpretation?
4. Is there a clear statement as to the grounds on which disciplinary action is to be pursued?

Case sheet 9: Statements by observers

Statement from Carlotta Mendez, The cook: 23.7.00

I was in the kitchen clearing up after tea. At about 8.00 p.m. I heard raised voices coming from the lounge, which is next door to the kitchen, although the door was closed and I was not able to see anything. I could not hear all the words being spoken in the argument. I then heard Brian shouting at Judy, calling her a 'fucking cow'. Judy then replied 'What the hell is your problem? Why are you being like this?' I then heard Judy crying and after this, I heard Sophie intervening and the conversation ended.

Statement from Brian Elder, RCO: 26.7.00

I came into work at 2.00 p.m. on Sunday 23rd July, feeling a bit down, because my girlfriend and I had broken up the day before. At about 8.00 p.m. Judy asked me to see about bathing Larry one of the residents for whom I'm keyworker. At that time, I explained that I was spending quality time with another resident, watching a film that I had promised to watch with them earlier in the shift. Judy started to ask me why I had been so quiet, and was I still with my girlfriend, Lisa. I said that was none of her business. She carried on about my attitude and said that I was really difficult to work with. I started to get angry. I can't remember what I said but I told her to leave me alone and I tried to leave the room but she got in my way and I might have pushed her as I went out through the door.

Sophie asked us to come with her to the office. She asked me what was going on with all the shouting and why was Judy in tears? I tried to explain what had been going on, but Judy just kept interrupting and crying. I was really getting angry by this point. I think I said something like 'I've had enough of bloody women'. At that point, Sophie asked me to calm down and talk about the problem, reminding me it was near the end of the shift and that it might be better if I went home. I thought this was the best plan of action and left the unit.

The next day I was feeling unwell and reported in sick. I returned to work three days later.

Statement from Judy Menzies, RCO: 23.7.00

I arrived for work at 2.00 p.m. this afternoon. I was on shift with Sophie, Brian and Billy. When Brian arrived, he appeared preoccupied and didn't acknowledge my 'Hello'. I have found it difficult to work with Brian in recent months. He has been increasingly moody and after he asked me out on a date and I said 'No', he has been quite hostile.

At about 7.30 p.m. this evening, Larry Stevens, one of the residents, was becoming quite agitated waiting for his bath which Brian was supposed to be giving him. I found Brian watching TV with another resident and when I pointed out that Larry was getting agitated waiting for his bath, Brian said not to take any notice, Larry always got a bit uptight but he would be OK. I left it half an hour but when I discovered that Larry was still waiting and getting distressed, I spoke to Brian again. This time he told me to leave him alone and got more angry towards me. He shouted 'you fucking cow' at me before pushing past me as he left the room, shoving me against the wall. I became quite upset at his attitude and started to cry.

Sophie intervened at this point. We were both asked to go to the office. Sophie wanted to know what the problem was. Brian started give his version of events but it just wasn't true and I became more upset. He became more angry and shouted at both of us that he was 'fed up with bloody women'. Sophie asked Brian to calm down so things could be sorted out, or he would be sent home. At this point Brian said 'That's fine by me' and stormed out, slamming the door with such force that he wrenched the handle.

I am submitting this report at the end of the shift to Sophie, my line manager.

Statement from Sophie Taylor, Team Leader and Shift Leader: 23.7.00

At 1.45 p.m. on Sunday 23rd July I arrived for work and went straight to the office. At the 2.00 p.m. handover I noticed a slight smell of alcohol on Brian's breath but I did not notice anything unusual about his behaviour, although he did appear quiet as he had for the past few shifts I have worked with him.

After the afternoon activities and tea, when it was quiet, I went to the office after informing the staff team that I was balancing the petty cash money. I ensured they understood that they could call me if needed.

After about ten minutes I heard raised voices from the lounge and Brian shouting loudly. I went out to the hall and found Judy still in the lounge in tears and Brian standing in the hallway, clearly very angry. Arthur, a resident, was sitting in the lounge looking rather frightened and upset. I called to Billy to sit with Arthur, while I asked Judy and Brian to come with me to the office.

I asked Judy and Brian what had happened. Brian started to say that Judy had been interfering with his work and asking questions about his personal life. Judy started to get even more upset, saying that Brian was not saying what had really happened. Brian got more angry and said 'I've had enough of bloody women'. I advised him to calm down and said that if he did not control himself I would be forced to send him off duty. He said that was fine by him and left the room in such a temper that he broke the handle as he slammed the door.

I asked Judy to make a written statement. Jill and Billy, the other two members of staff on duty have also made statements, which are attached with my own.

Statement from Billy O'Connell, RCO: 23.7.00

I reported for duty at 2.00 p.m. on 23.7.96. It was an uneventful shift until there was a commotion in the lounge at around 8.00 p.m. I had been assisting Clive with the toilet when I heard raised voices which sounded like Judy and Brian coming from the lounge. Brian was shouting, Judy was crying. I heard Sophie call for me. Clive had finished, so I went to the lounge and was asked to sit with Arthur, who was clearly distressed. While I was sitting with him, he said that he thought it was his fault. He wanted Brian to watch the film with him but he was frightened when Brian became so angry with Judy. He thought that Brian must have really hurt Judy to make her cry. He said that Judy had been cross with Brian because Larry was waiting for his bath, but that Brian had not taken any notice of her, which in the beginning he was quite pleased about.

I spent half an hour with Arthur, reassuring him it was not his fault and that he was not to be frightened as Sophie was dealing with the situation.

Statement from Olive Newsom, Team Leader (Supervisor to Brian Elder): 25.7.00

I have supervised Brian Elder for over twelve months. He has been for much of that time a caring and conscientious member of staff, who relates well to the residents.

However, we have discussed in supervision some of the problems he has, in working with certain members of staff. Brian likes to work independently and can find it difficult to work with others, and we have spent a good deal of time looking at the importance of a team approach.

I have become more concerned in the last two months as Brian seems to have become rather depressed, showing less interest in his work and complaining more bitterly about individual members of staff, in particular Judy Menzies. He finds her a very forceful personality which he has difficulty in coping with. I was getting to the point of recommending that Brian considered counselling, before this incident occurred. I am aware that Brian has also been experiencing problems with his girlfriend (he has arrived late on several occasions after they have had a row) although he has not felt that it was relevant to discuss this in supervision. I did of course point out that he had a duty to report for work on time whatever his personal circumstances.

There has been no suggestion that Brian has any alcohol problem either when I have worked with him, or during supervision sessions.

Training module: Recording a supervisory interview

 **Objective**

The aim of the module is to apply the principles of good recording to a supervisory interview. Learners are asked to write the record of the supervision, from a transcript on the case sheet.

Timing

Allow 45 minutes for this module.

Materials

You will need:

- case sheet 10: *Transcript: Recording a supervisory interview*
- paper
- pens

Trainer's guidelines

Step 1: allow 25 minutes

Explain the purpose of the exercise, and divide the participants into groups of three or four. Distribute the case sheet to all the learners, before asking them to write the record of the supervisory interview as if they were the supervisor.

Step 2: allow 20 minutes

Ask each group to read out their supervision record and then discuss each record with the whole group. Review the records in terms of:

- Was the main purpose of the supervision, i.e. that it was the probationary period review, clearly identified?
- Were the main areas of concern identified, i.e. punctuality, and failure to understand teamwork and the key-working system?
- Were the positive areas identified, i.e. enthusiasm and commitment, forming of good relationships with residents?
- Was the issue of punctuality sufficiently dealt with, i.e. lateness not acceptable, necessary for supervisee to resolve her travel problems?
- Were the means of resolution of the teamwork problems adequately described, i.e. through more frequent supervision?
- Was the supervisee's interest in further training included, along with the supervisor's response?
- Was a clear statement made about recommending an extension of the probationary period?

Case sheet 10: Transcript: Recording a supervisory interview

Setting: Residential home for the elderly

Helen: (Supervisor) *Come in Julie, sit down. Would you like a cup of coffee?*

Julie: (Supervisee) *No thanks, I only had one half an hour ago.*

Helen: *Well Julie, you are coming to the end of your probationary period, and it's important that we take this opportunity to review your progress over the last six months. How do you feel yourself about how you've got on?*

Julie: *Well, I'm quite pleased really. I mean, when I started I hadn't done this sort of work before. I wasn't sure whether it was something I would be any good at, but I really get on well with the residents, and I feel I'm doing something a lot more worthwhile than when I was working with the building society.*

Helen: *Yes, you have made great efforts in establishing some very positive relationships with the residents. However, we have discussed in previous supervisions, the importance of working as part of a team and recognising the role of the keyworker in relation to individual residents. Some staff have found it difficult, and residents have become confused when you have assumed responsibilities and tasks with some residents that were more properly the job of their keyworker.*

Julie: *Well yes, I know, but as I've said before, it's very hard when you really get on well with some of the residents and they ask you to do something, especially when they complain their keyworker hasn't bothered. I mean Mrs Ramsden is so sweet, I don't mind doing a little bit extra. It's not like she has any family that comes to visit her regularly anyway.*

Helen: *Your concern and interest with Mrs Ramsden is evidence of your caring and commitment, but it can also cause problems when you forget that you are part of a team, where every member of staff has something to contribute, and people need to understand each others' roles and responsibilities.*
            Anyway Julie, I think it would be a good idea if I outlined the areas I think we need to discuss this morning.

Julie: *OK. Will I have a chance to raise any issues myself?*

Helen: *Of course. I hope you feel you've always been able to bring any concerns to these sessions. Anyway, as far as this morning is concerned, I think we need to explore further your understanding of working as part of a team. I also have a lot of concern over your punctuality which has not really been satisfactory. Both of these issues are important and will be factors in my decision over whether you pass your probationary period or not.*

Julie: *I know I've had a lot of problems with the bus, but as I've said before, that's not my fault.*

Helen: *Let's discuss that in a minute. I would like to discuss the positives first. It is clear that you enjoy your work here, and you show great enthusiasm in the way you approach different aspects of your work. You relate very well to the residents and you have managed to form some very good relationships with even the most withdrawn residents. This suggests a very good base from which to start. Clearly you are finding this work more fulfilling than your previous job, and that is important. It can be difficult work, and at times very emotionally draining, and unless you are really motivated it can be hard.*

Julie: *I just wish that I'd realised earlier how much I'd enjoy this work and not wasted so much time at college getting all those secretarial qualifications. It was all a bit pointless. I would have been better studying for something more relevant to what I'm doing now. That's one of the things I wanted to talk to you about. I really would like the chance to go for further training. I know I've done the induction and some of the short courses, but I'd really like to go for professional training.*

Helen: *Well, it's good that you want to get on. However, it is increasingly difficult for us as a department to support staff for professional training, and priority normally would go to people who had been with us a little longer.*

Anyway, to get back to my original points. I really do need to raise again with you, Julie, the issue of your lateness. I know you've blamed the buses but at the end of the day, it is your responsibility to get yourself here on time. It's part of working as a team, to be there, when you are expected. Your lateness has meant that other staff have not been able to leave until you have arrived, sometimes as much as forty-five minutes late. In the six months you've been with us you have arrived late on over twenty occasions.

Julie: *I have been trying to sort it out, but the buses are so unreliable. They only have to cut one out and I have to wait another half an hour for the next one. It's all right for people with cars, they only have to jump in and they're off, but it's not so easy when you have to rely on public transport. And I can't afford to buy a car. I can't even drive anyway.*

Helen: *Well, we have talked about you coming on a bike. The journey is only five miles after all.*

Julie: *My Mum wouldn't have me riding a bike. When I told her you'd suggested that, she nearly went spare. My cousin was knocked over when she was only twelve. There's no way you'd get me on a bike, not with the roads around here.*

Helen: *Well, we do have a problem then Julie, because somehow or other you have got to sort out your transport problems so that you can be here on time. How you do that, is really up to you. But I cannot allow the present situation to continue.*

Julie: *I don't think you're being fair but I really don't want to lose this job. Give me a bit more time and I'll think of something.*

Helen: *As I said earlier, there is another issue which we have discussed in previous supervisions. It's about your difficulty in recognising that you are working as part of a team. You need to be aware of where you fit into the team, rather than going off on your own, with what might seem like a good idea to you, but which may be, because you don't discuss it with anyone, and you are inexperienced, inappropriate, and undermining of the work of someone else. Also, it's important that we keep one another informed so that we can co-ordinate what we're doing and how we're working with particular residents. This issue has been covered in your training and in discussion with me during supervision.*

Julie: *I know sometimes I've got a bit carried away, but honestly some of the other staff are not the easiest people to work with. Just because you're new they treat you as though you're stupid, especially if you're a lot younger than them. I have tried, but they don't make it easy, and Mary has had it in for me ever since I arrived.*

Helen: *Being able to work with different colleagues, even the ones we don't especially like, is all part of learning to do the job, and part of developing a more mature approach to your work.*

Julie: *But they did say on one of the courses, that if we had any concerns about how the residents were being treated, then we needed to report it, because too much has gone on in the past in residential homes, and staff just kept quiet about it.*

Helen: *Of course it's important for staff to speak out, when it's necessary, but I don't think we're talking about abuse or neglect in relation to this home, Julie. Your inexperience sometimes means you don't always understand why it is important to maintain professional boundaries. You mistake that for not always caring, and do not always appreciate why staff are working with a resident in a particular way.*

Julie: *I want to learn, and that's why I want more training.*

Helen: *It's not just a question of attending training. It's about listening to what people are trying to say to you. At the moment Julie, I do not feel able to say that you have successfully completed your probationary period. Your lateness, and lack of appreciation of what it means to work as a team, are the principal reasons. However, I do acknowledge your high level of commitment to the work and for this reason I have decided to recommend that your probationary period be extended for a further three months. During that time I would offer fortnightly supervision in an effort to address these problems with you. I should say though, that the problem of lateness is yours to sort out. I shall simply be monitoring that situation. On the other issue, I would hope that with some specific work we may be able to make some progress.*

Julie: *I have to say I'm disappointed. I had hoped that my probationary period would be over but I suppose if you feel like that, then I have to accept it. I do hear what you're saying but it's still difficult for me.*

Helen: *Thank you Julie, and I'll let you know the outcome of my recommendation.*